*THE TOUGHEST MEN IN SPORTS:*
*Looking for the Mental Edge*


*A publication of*
*Culture House Books – March 2001*

*For information address:*      *Culture House*
                                *P O Box 293*
                                *Newton, IA 50208*


*Library of Congress Catalog Card Number:*
*83-80730*

*ISBN: 0-9676080-1-5*
*(previously published by Leisure Press, ISBN 0-88011-187-9)*

*Cover design by: Terry Down*
*Cover illustration by: Jack Bender*

# THE
# TOUGHEST MEN
## IN
# SPORTS

## LOOKING FOR THE MENTAL EDGE

MIKE CHAPMAN

*Mike Chapman*

**CULTURE HOUSE BOOKS**

*"There is no greater glory for a man
as long as he lives
than that which he wins
by his own hands and feet."*

Homer, The Odyssey

# CONTENTS

# ACKNOWLEDGMENTS

Nearly every book is a collection of thoughts, observations and interactions in which a great number of people play a substantial part. *The Toughest Men in Sports* is certainly no exception. Among those who have played a prominent role in the development of this book are Ken Taylor, Jim Duschen, Tim Williams, Randy Grenz, Bud Pearson, Randy Lewis, Mark Johnson, Tom Burns, Gil Hansen, Dan Gable, Dan Rowray, Dan Goddard, Denny Young, Roy Douglas, Mike Narey, Vic Marcucci, Tom Peckham, Jim Kinyon, Reefer Clagg, Matt Clarke, Joe Bittner, Steve Shrock, Dan Hodge, Verne Gagne, Pat O'Connor, Maury Hachey, Steve Eden, Lou Banach, Steve DeVries, Don Buzzard, Gene Butler, Paul Widmayer, Larry Bedard, Jim Scheppele, Rich Somodi and Chuck Yesalis. They are all tough men, in one way or another. Special thanks also go to Clark Beltz and Jack Bender for the cover design, and to David R. Kauss, author of *Peak Performance*, and Thomas Tutko, author of *Sports Psyching*. Their books offered excellent reading. I must also acknowledge the excellent editorial work of *The Ring* and *KO Magazine*, two sources from which I drew a great deal of the references contained in this work. Another special thanks is due Terry Merriman, who set up for me a long, personal interview with Bill Wallace. And, as always, my greatest appreciation is reserved for my wife, Beverly, who somehow manages to listen to all my thoughts and ramblings, and then agrees to put them down on paper for me. Her patience and understanding are on-going, and seemingly endless . . .

# FOREWORD

In all the years I've been involved in athletics, one man has clearly stood above all the rest in terms of his pure knowledge of sports. Mike Chapman is a true athlete's sportswriter, one who is not only dedicated to his work, but enthusiastic about it. He has successfully participated in judo and wrestling, and he bench presses an amazing 440 pounds. With over fifteen years of experience in covering the sports world and as sports editor of the second-largest newspaper in Iowa, Chapman has received numerous honors and awards. His most recent honor was being chosen Grand Marshal of the dual wrestling meet between the Soviet Union and the United States. He has twice been named national wrestling sportswriter of the year, the highest award in his field.

Boxing, wrestling and the martial arts are his specialty, and having published numerous articles in all three areas, he has compiled enough facts and figures to make any historian envious. His personal library of books and films on these sports is endless. While discussing any subject, Chapman consistently supports his statements with facts, not opinions. His book, *The Toughest Men In Sports*, is a tribute to some of the most courageous men ever—men who, in turn, should feel privileged to be in a book written by such a true sportswriter.

It has been an honor to know this man and call him my friend.

*MARK JOHNSON*
*Member 1980 Olympic wrestling team*
*Assistant wrestling coach, University of Iowa*

# INTRODUCTION

# Searching for the Mental Edge

Over three thousand years ago, on a faraway, wind-swept plain, before a proud city, the two greatest warriors in all of history and literature prepared to fight to the death. For ten long years, their respective armies had struggled valiantly, the advantage shifting from side to side as wheat blowing into the wind. Yet these two magnificent warriors had never before faced one another on the field of combat.

Men—those too old for battle and soldiers in the very prime of their lives—stood on the high walls of the beseiged city as the spectacle unfolded beneath them. Women shrieked and pulled their hair in fear and frustration. Even the gods and goddesses on nearby Mount Olympus, it is said, grew silent and watchful, eagerly anticipating the spectacular event that was about to take place before their very eyes. The plain was called the Troad, and the city was known as Troy. It stood at the mouth of the Hellespont at the northeastern tip of the Aegean Sea, the spot where the culture of ancient Greece collided with that of Asia Minor. The combatants were Achilles and Hector—names that would survive thirty centuries. All of them were destined for immortality, thanks to a blind poet named Homer who created the epic poems, *The Iliad and The Odyssey*. The first described in full and gory details the wrath of Achilles and the battle at Troy; the second told of the Herculean struggles of one man to return to his homeland after ten years of war at Troy.

Achilles represented the very finest of the invading army. The legends told of his birth to a sea goddess named Thetis, and how she, holding him by the heel, had dipped him in the River Styx in the Land of the Dead, to make him immortal. He was raised in the mountainous high country in the kingdom of Pythia, in northern Thessaly. His tutor was, they said, the man-horse Cheiron, of the race of centaurs. According to the great

8

mythographer Robert Graves, Cheiron fed him "on the umbles of lions and wild boars, and the marrow of bears, to give him courage . . . and fawns' marrow to make him run swiftly." He was the epitome of the Greek warrior—a man without peer in combat.

Troy hoped to find his match in the reboubtable Hector, the eldest son of King Priam. Known as the horse-tamer, Hector fought with a wild intensity and courage that knew few limits. He was powerful, according to Homer, and highly skilled with the short sword and the spear, the primary fighting weapons of the day. For ten years, he was the pride of Troy. He was its heart, its backbone, its very spirit.

The day these two magnificent warriors were fated to meet, only Hector dared to venture out beyond the safety of Troy's walls. Once, on an earlier occasion when Achilles had shown himself to the Trojan army—though naked and weaponless—the soldiers of Troy had fled the field even though he had but shaken his fist and shouted out his name. Somehow, Hector had summoned the courage to meet Achilles in single combat; yet, that same courage just as suddenly betrayed him at the last moment. As he saw his foe advancing, his golden armor shining in the mid-day sun, Hector ran. Three times he circled the walls of Troy, Achilles in hot pursuit. Finally, Troy's greatest son stood his ground and spoke to the terrible, death-dealing Achilles, trying to bargain—"to set the duel within the intelligible limits of humanity," wrote Cedric H. Whitman in his book, *Homer and the Heroic Tradition,* "let them guarantee each other decent burial, whoever conquers." But Achilles no longer knew humanity and appropriately enough retorted in images of wild animals:

*Hector, speak not to me, ruinous wretch, of agreements,*
*As between lions and men there are no sacred oaths,*
*Neither do wolves and sheep have like tempers,*
*So between you and me no friendship.*

"The battle is," wrote Whitman, "in terms which Hector has never before conceived."

The confrontation between Achilles and Hector is perhaps the single most dramatic, conclusive, and tragic battle ever recorded. Achilles slays Hector quickly, driving a spear through his neck, and , with the citizens of Troy watching helplessly from the battlements, drags his lifeless body behind his chariot back and forth before the walls of Troy.

Achilles and Hector have both survived the ages, however, earning true immortality. Thirty centuries after their passing, students around the world read of their deeds and study their actions. Homer also lives on in the libraries of man, regarded by many as the greatest story teller who ever lived. No person has yet matched his narrative skill when it comes to

**9**

depicting man against man in the epic battle for survival. As a chronicler of war, he stands paramount.

But it was Whitman who took us to the very heart of the issue. It was Whitman who grasped the essence of the confrontation, telling us that "the battle is in terms which Hector has never before conceived." The supremacy of Achilles culminated in a physical verification, but it had its origins deep in the minds of both Achilles and Hector. Achilles' will was forged with steel; he had seen his beloved friend Patroclus killed by Hector in combat. In his overwhelming grief, he discovered a new Achilles, a man who could, and would, commit his entire being, his very existence, to one goal . . . the destruction of Hector. Whatever doubts he may have had prior to facing Hector were erased, completely and forever, by his consuming passion for revenge.

Hector approached the inevitable contest with growing concern and trepidation. His parents and friends begged him not to face an angry Achilles, fearing he would most certainly lose, and die. In one of the most touching and human scenes in all of literature, his wife, Andromache, bearing their tiny son, approaches Hector at the gates of the city and pleads with him not to face Achilles. Achilles has slain her father and brothers, she tells her husband, but while Hector lives they all live for her—in Hector.

Hector is filled with doubts, and why not? Even his loved ones have given up hope for his success, acknowledging that he is fighting a superior warrior. His courage rises and falls, and he at last displays his own feelings about the outcome when he attempts to bargain with Achilles. It is the last desperate act of a man who knows he is lost, and Achilles seizes the opportunity to further decrease Hector's chances of victory with a crushing response.

Achilles not only stands tall as the greatest warrior in all of recorded history, but he also emerges as the first to realize the mental edge. He, in essence, gained his victory before the first spear was even thrown. He had only to close out the scene with the physical reality. It is a scenario that would be repeated a hundred, a thousand, and even a million times in the centuries that followed, and it is a victory that still echoes throughout twentieth century America, where most battles are relegated to sports arenas.

Wherever men gather to test themselves in one-on-one combat, the lesson of Achilles versus Hector will be replayed—to greater or lesser degrees. For contests for supremacy on the very highest levels are waged not physically, but mentally. When the very best boxers step into the ring to struggle for championships, when the world's greatest wrestlers lock arms, when the finest martial artists square off, the contests will be determined, in most instances, by the mental edges of the winners. They will exhibit and call upon that certain something—that heretofore indefinable quality, that intangible substance—from which winners are fashioned.

"There is something special in the makeup of top amateurs," said Bob Kane, a former president of the United States Olympic Committee, in 1982.

There is also something special in the makeup of all the world's top athletes, particularly those who elect to compete in the demanding realm of one-on-one, where there are no teammates to come to one's side, and where there is nowhere to hide—for even a moment.

"I can tell when an athlete has got it, in most cases," said a longtime follower of amateur wrestling. "I can see it in his eyes. It's that certain something, something special, and something mental."

All super athletes have been blessed with the physical necessities to become great. They have the required genes, which provide them with a base and the opportunity to rise to the very pinnacle of success. They have access, for the most part, to the same kinds of training facilities, teachers, methods, schools, and nutritional sources—at least in a relative sense. Yet some excel, going on to become world and Olympic champions, while others are incapable of climbing the very highest mountain, of standing on the summit. The difference, it seems safe to suggest, is mental. It lies deep within the essence of the individual warrior. Perhaps it can be brought to the surface, nurtured and cultured. Perhaps it cannot. Perhaps that certain something, the mental edge, can be taught and transmitted; perhaps not. But we can study it nonetheless. We can observe instances of supreme mental conditioning, and try to understand and utilize what we learn. Perhaps by looking into the actions of the greatest champions of American one-on-one sports we can come to terms with what the mental edge is, and how it operates. That will be the task of this book. In these pages, the reader may catch a glimpse of that magical world of competition as seen through the accomplishments and thoughts of some of the toughest men in sports. We will meet the savage Jack Dempsey, the obsessed Dan Gable, the mythical Bruce Lee and other magnificent heroes of one-on-one. Through them, we will search for that elusive mental edge—the quality that made the difference in the great confrontation between Achilles and Hector over three thousand years ago—and perhaps learn how to apply it in our lives today.

With hair shaved high above his ears and wearing several days' worth of whiskers, a scowling Jack Dempsey awaits the start of his bout with huge Jess Willard on July 4, 1919. Dempsey demolished Willard to win the world title.

# JACK DEMPSEY

# The Savage Beast

If ever a man was born to fight, it was William Harrison (Jack) Dempsey. Entering the world on June 24, 1895, in the out-of-the-way western town of Manassa, Colorado, he stormed through the boxing ranks in a style that had never been seen before and has not been duplicated since.

He earned his fighting spurs in the rough mining towns of the West, and fought for peanuts. He would take on anyone, anytime, anywhere, for just about any price.

He has been called by experts the most savage man ever to climb into the prize ring . . . an animal uncaged, a wild beast intent upon devouring his victim with ferocity almost beyond human comprehension.

Nat Fleischer, the founder and publisher of *The Ring* magazine, and the nation's greatest authority on boxing, ranked Jack Dempsey the best puncher in the history of boxing, regardless of size, era or style. Fleischer also ranked Dempsey number one in the categories of "best infighter" and "most killer instinct."

"It is doubtful if any heavyweight before or since could have surpassed Jack Dempsey's pure savagery in the ring," wrote Graham Houston in the book *Superfists*. "His style was one of unbridled aggression and he was called The Manassa Mauler for a good reason."

The editors of *Boxing Legends* magazine said it this way: "Stubble-chinned, scowling, mean, Dempsey attacked opponents with a non-stop ferocity never seen before or since."

That's the legacy of Jack Dempsey. In the 1980s, more than fifty years since Dempsey last had a serious fight, the name still has a magic quality, a folk-hero ring to it. Dempsey was of the same period as Babe Ruth, Jim Thorpe, Big Bill Tilden and Red Grange. At his peak, which lasted for over seven years, he was the most idolized athlete in America. One can build a good case for Dempsey being the most popular sports figure of all time.

THE CHICAGO DAILY TRIBUNE: SATURDAY, JULY 5, 1919.

# DEMPSEY WINS WORLD TITLE WITH SCIENCE AS WELL AS POWER

## STUDIES RIVAL UNTIL CERTAIN, THEN TEARS IN

**Crowd Is Surprised by Methods Used by New Champ.**

BY RAY PEARSON.

## THE NEW CHAMPION

*"Well, Gents, Just a Practical Joke, Me Picking Jess," Says Ring Lardner*

BY RING W. LARDNER

## DEMPSEY GLAD; READY TO FIGHT TO HOLD TITLE

**Speed of Victory Delights New Champ and He Calls for More.**

BY WALTER ECKERSALL.

## In the Wake of the News
### By JACK LAIT

### THE NEW CHAMP, HOW HE CLIMBED TO FISTIC HONORS FROM MINES

### CHICAGO DEMPSEYS, THOUSAND STRONG, REJOICE OVER NEWS

BY JOHN KELLEY

## JESS WILLARD'S WIFE SEES HIM LOSE THE CROWN

**'Glad He's Ex-Champion'; Helps Him Care for Wounds.**

### Cool, Fizzy Home-made Drink

Paul Gallico, one of the country's best-known writers a generation ago, said that Jack Dempsey was "the greatest and most beloved sports hero the country had ever known."

In 1950, the sportswriters of the nation voted him the third best male athlete of the first half centry. Only Jim Thorpe and Babe Ruth captured more support from the voters.

Rex Lardner, in his classic book, *The Legendary Champions*, wrote that Dempsey ". . . was certainly the most exciting, the most colorful, the most dynamic and the most savage (fighter who ever lived). There was an immense fury coiled inside him waiting to be released."

And yet, there is another side to Dempsey. It is a side that is in total contrast to the caged animal evidenced in the ring. By nearly all accounts, Dempsey was an exceedingly friendly and gentle soul outside of the ring. He always wore a big smile, was open and easy-going with strangers, and could charm a fellow out of his eye teeth.

Grantland Rice, the most revered sportswriter of all time, summed up the Dempsey contradiction brilliantly: "Dempsey was the oddest mixture of humanity I've known," offered Rice. "In the ring he was a killer—a superhuman wild man. His teeth were frequently bared and his complete intent was an opponent's destruction. He was a fighter—one who used every trick to wreck the other fighter. Yet, outside the ring, Jack is one of the gentlest men I know. I've known the man closely for more than thirty years and I've never seen him in a rough argument or as anything except courteous and considerate."

Dempsey had what many other great fighters had but to a lesser degree . . . an innate ability to turn his savage self off and on like a light switch. Dempsey was able to work himself into a killer rage, but he confined the rage to the ring. In his ability to trigger and control the fire inside, Dempsey stands unique in the history of sports.

"The way I've lived it, fighting isn't planning or figuring," said Dempsey, decades after his last bout. "It's all instinct. You rip, you tear, you slash. You're not thinking of winning by strategy. You're moved by only one thing—the instinct to survive."

To understand Dempsey, one has to understand his origins. He was the ninth of thirteen children, born into a family in the grip of abject poverty. The Dempseys moved from spot to spot in Colorado and Utah, barely having enough money to keep food on the table. At fifteen, young Jack and his older brother Bernie made a small gym out of an old chicken coop and began training. In his autobiography, Dempsey said his mother, Celia, "a tough, wiry little woman . . . was responsible for instilling the fight in me, for her great hero was the famous old heavyweight boxing champion, John L. Sullivan."

Jack and Bernie worked to develop their wind by racing against one of the family horses, and Jack even went to the lengths of chewing pine gum

# The Chicago

THE WORLD'S GREATEST

VOLUME LXXVIII.—NO. 160. C. [COPYRIGHT: 1919: BY THE TRIBUNE COMPANY.] SATURDAY, JU

# DEMPSEY W

## JESS WILLARD QUITS AS 4TH ROUND STARTS

### Tosses Up Sponge After Terrific Beating.

BY HARVEY T. WOODRUFF.

Bay View Park Arena, Toledo, O., July 4.—(Special.) — Jack Dempsey is world's heavyweight champion.

It took this modern David just three rounds to usurp the title and dissipate all claims of Jess Willard, the contemporaneous Goliath at Bay View Park Arena this afternoon.

### White Flag Is Hoisted.

Never before in the history of the heavyweight crown has a title holder accepted such concentrated punishment as Jack the giant killer meted out in those nine minutes of milling before the seconds of the champion tossed a towel into the ring.

The accepted white flag of surrender in fistiana was raised shortly before time would have been called for the fourth round.

Whatever else may be said of Willard, his gameness can never be questioned. Fifty seconds after the bout started he was upset by one of Dempsey's left hooks,

## FIGHT PICTURES TO THE TRIBUNE BY AIRPLANE

A set of photographic views of the Dempsey-Willard fight is published on page 7, showing in detail the progress of the battle. These pictures were brought to Chicago in a government mail airplane and delivered to "The Tribune" office at 8 p. m. A photograph of the plane arriving in Grant park appears on page 3.

The mail parcels containing the photographic plates bore the postmark "Toledo, 5:15 p. m.," and reached the landing field on the lake front, Chicago, at 7:53. The elapsed flying time was two hours and thirty-eight minutes, and the distance covered was approximately 244 miles—over ninety-three miles an hour.

Six hours after the fight ended an early edition of "The Tribune," containing the pictures, was on sale in Chicago.

In addition to the courtesies extended by the government air mail authorities, "The Tribune" is indebted to George W. Browne, western manager of the Curtiss Aero company, and Vice President and General Sales Manager Edwin W. Jackson of the Willys-Overland company for co-operation in the air flights.

## WILLARD SCARED STIFF, OPINION OF PERCY HAMMOND

COMPETITIO

[Copyright: 1919: By John T. McCut

THE BIG TWO

WILLARD-DEMPSEY FIGHT

## THE WEATHER

SATURDAY, JULY 5, 1919.

Sunrise, 5:20 a. m.; sunset, 8:25 p. m. Moon sets 12:29 a. m. Sunday.

Chicago and vicinity:
Fair and considerably cooler today; tomorrow fair, with moderate temperature; moderate north to northeast winds.

Illinois—Generally fair and cooler in north, thundershowers and cooler in south today; tomorrow fair,

## TRAIN KILLS 5 IN CHICAGO AU

Engine Hits the Ma
Squarely at De
Rav. Ill.

# aily Tribune.

**NEWSPAPER**

1919.—22 PAGES. TWO SECTIONS SECTION ONE  **PRICE TWO CENTS** IN CHICAGO AND SUBURBS

# NS; SIX KNOCKDOWNS IN THREE MINUTES

"ARE THEY FIGHTING FOR POINTS OR A DECISION?"

## LORD SUMNER TO PRESIDE IN KAISER TRIAL

### Holland to Make No Fight on Yielding Ex-Emperor.

LONDON, July 5, 8 a. m.—The allies, according to the Daily Mail, have received assurances that the government of Holland in the last resort will not refuse to surrender the former German emperor for trial.

The newspaper says that the necessary formal objections will doubtless be raised to maintain the rights of Dutch sovereignty, but, as the demand for his person can be made in the name of the league of nations, national rights will not be infringed, and there is no doubt the Dutch government will be ready to get rid of the unwelcome guest.

The chief count in the former kaiser's indictment, the Mail understands, will be his action in causing violation of Belgium and Luxembourg. The proceeding will be conducted in English, but a translation will be made into several languages simultaneously.

**Lord Sumner to Preside.**

John Andrew Hamilton, Lord Sumner will preside over the five judges representing the United States, Great Britain, France, Italy, and Japan at the trial of the former German emperor, according to the Evening News.

Sir Gordon Hewart, solicitor general of Great Britain, will lead for the prosecution. William Hohenzollern, it is said, will be defended by German counsel, assisted by British lawyers if he wishes them.

It is thought here that the American representative on the tribunal will be

## ATE NEWS BULLETINS

RIS, July 4.—The undersecretary of state for demobilization, replying to an interpellation in the chamber of deputies today, said that mobilization of all reservists in army will be completed Oct. 30. lists and Republican Socialists anded that the reservists be sent a month earlier. The chamen approved the government's

## Joffre Tells of Terrible Days at Start

PARIS, July 4.—[By the Associated Press.]—Marshal Joffre appeared before the chamber of deputies committee of investigation of the metal industries during the war today and replied to criticisms made before the committee by certain generals of the failure to defend the Briey iron mining district and the failure to provide for an attack by the Germans through Belgium.

The Briey basin, the marshal said, was not included in the covering positions because it was impossible to prevent the Germans from taking it. The plans of the general staff were made to follow every step of the invasion with the end in view of not engaging in battle until it could do so with a totality of forces, which, at the beginning, were 2,300,000 bayonets.

British military aid was provided for, Marshal Joffre told the commission, in a secret military agreement. He said he had counted upon six English divisions. Referring to the defeat at Charleroi, the marshal declared it was the most terrible day of his existence.

Generals who were his best friends were broken because they were not equal to their task, in consequence of which certain units fell back in disorder. Marshal Joffre explained that the abandonment of Lille was because it could not be defended.

## MANY KILLED IN AN ACCIDENT TO EXCURSION BOAT

Sioux Falls, S. D., July 4.—Between ten and fifteen people are reported to have drowned when an excursion boat on Lake Madison, about forty miles northwest of this city, struck a snag and overturned tonight.

Only meager reports have been received. The boat is said to have turned completely over twice and then sunk

## DIRIGIBLE PAST SYDNEY IN DASH FOR NEW YORK

### Gives Up Attempt to Reach St. Johns, Is Report.

**BULLETIN.**

Halifax, N. S., July 4.—The Handley-Page bombing plane, bound from Harbor Grace, N. F., for Atlantic City, N. J., passed over Antigonish, N. S., at 11:45 tonight, local time. The plane was traveling at high speed and at a great height. Antigonish is 120 miles east of Halifax.

Sydney, N. S., July 4.—The British dirigible R-34, en route to America from Scotland, passed over Sydney at 9 p. m., local time, tonight, according to wireless messages picked up at Louisburg and Glace bay and transmitted here.

It is just possible that the R-34 and the Handley-Page bombing plane which started for Atlantic City, N. J., from Harbor Grace, N. F., this afternoon, met each other at sea this evening. Both craft were reported fifty miles off this city at 8:40 o'clock (New York time).

**Abandons Trip to St. Johns.**

St. Johns, N. F., July 4.—At 9 o'clock Greenwich time the wireless station at Mount Pearl reported that the R-34 had abandoned its attempt to reach St Johns and was proceeding westward from Trinity bay, headed in the direction of New York.

A later message received at the admiralty wireless station here states the R-34 was headed for the Canadian mainland and making good progress "straight from the trees" to try and strengthen his jaw. In addition, he soaked his face in beef brine in an attempt to toughen his skin.

Dempsey "graduated" from eighth grade—a level of education reached by only one other member of his immediate family—and at sixteen left home to try and make a living. He began working as a miner, and the hard work helped to harden his already lean and thickly-muscled body into a perfect fighting machine. For five years he alternated the two activities, boxing and mining, and he worked in every type of mine available.

Fighting under the name "Kid Blackie," Dempsey rode the railways of the era living a hobo life and looking for pickup fights anywhere he could find them. Said Dempsey, "Back in Colorado, I got fights by walking into saloons and announcing, with what I hoped was the grand eloquence of the great John L. Sullivan, 'I can't sing and I can't dance, but I'll lick anyone in the house.' Sometimes I wasn't taken seriously because of my high-pitched voice, which got even more ridiculous whenever I was nervous or unsure of myself. Nevertheless, I never lost my nerve."

Times were tough. Some fights netted only a buck or two. If Kid Blackie lost, which wasn't often, there wasn't any money at all. Dempsey's opportunity to eat often rested on his ability to win. It was little wonder that Dempsey's size hovered around the 160-pound mark, and that he developed a real hunger to win. It was the only way to quiet the other hunger that was always gnawing at him.

Though Dempsey admits he often dreamed of being champion as a youngster, it was the dream of decent paydays that kept him fighting through the lean years he experienced in his late teens. In January of 1916, Dempsey landed a match with Boston Bearcat, a huge man who had reputedly given a stiff fight to the legendary black fighter, Sam Langford. Dempsey was leery of the Bearcat but took the fight anyway, and flattened the much larger man in just one round. It was a monumental win for the young Dempsey.

"Above all, I really got to know myself, to know my ability to take a blow and to know the extent of my endurance under different conditions," he said. "Missing a target only weakened my strength; it was better to duck, feint and weave. I practiced ducking my head from side to side when charging in, making me harder to hit."

It was the beginning of the development of the skill that would cause Fleischer to rank Dempsey the best infighter of all time. Shortly after the Bearcat fight, Dempsey was taken under the wing of Jack "Doc" Kearns, one of the most clever managers and promoters in the history of the sport. Kearns was impressed with Dempsey's non-stop style and punching power, and the two made a perfect combination. Together they would rise to the very top of the fistic world, bring in boxing's first million dollar gates, and make Dempsey a household word—a name that would, in time, eclipse even that of Sullivan.

Dempsey's reputation as "Jack the Giant Killer" got off the floor when he scored a spectacular knockout over Fred Fulton—six foot five and a leading title contender—in the unbelievable time of eighteen seconds. Shortly after that demolition job, Dempsey flattened another leading contender, six foot four Carl Morris . . . also in one round. The knockout of Morris and the feared Gunboat Smith, in two rounds, came at the end of 1918. The next year, 1919, was one of Dempsey's greatest, and led him to the world heavyweight boxing championship.

Dempsey fought six times in 1919, for a total of eight rounds. He stopped Big Jack Hickey, Kid Harris, Kid Henry, Eddy Smith and Tony Drake all in one round each. The next man managed to go three rounds, but he still lost several teeth and his crown. His name was Jess Willard, and his destruction by Dempsey was the most awesome dismantling of a champion in ring history.

The two men met in the stifling 110 degree heat of July 4, 1919, in Toldeo, Ohio. Dempsey, standing six foot one, weighed in at 180 pounds—sixty-seven pounds less than the six foot six, 247-pound Willard. Jess had put the white man back on the boxing throne by knocking out the great Jack Johnson four years earlier in Havana, Cuba. He was a big, tough man, but he was unprepared for the savage onslaught that he was to face in Toledo.

Dempsey started the fight slowly, not charging across the ring in his customary style. But just moments into the fight, the real Dempsey surfaced.

"Suddenly he exploded," wrote Lardner. "He charged forward . . . and shot a wilting right to the heart, then swung the left hook that poets should write about. It hit Willard in the jaw and broke it in seven places. Willard went down, got up and, with Dempsey standing over him, was smashed down again. The next time he got up, Dempsey tore in, hitting body, jaw, eye, mouth. Willard went down seven times, and the last time—four teeth missing, jaw broken, eye closed, bleeding from the nose—he could not get up."

Dempsey later said he knew the fight was over as soon as he landed his first devastating left hook. "I saw his cheekbone cave in," said Dempsey. It was the most devastating single round performance in boxing history. Willard was dragged back to his corner by his assistants, and Dempsey left the ring thinking he was the world champion. But the bell had sounded to end round one before Willard was counted out, and Dempsey had to be called back into the ring. He made it just in time to start round two, and the battering continued. Somehow, Willard lasted through rounds two and three, but he couldn't answer the bell for the fourth. Jack Dempsey was the heavyweight champion of the entire world.

**Heavyweight boxing champion of the world, Jess Willard (right), retreats under the ferocious attack of a snarling Jack Dempsey during the first round of their title clash in Toledo, Ohio, on July 4, 1919. In the stifling heat, the tigerish Dempsey demolished the huge Willard, knocking him down a total of seven times in the first round, breaking his jaw and knocking out four of his teeth. Willard, who stood six foot six and outweighed Dempsey by sixty-seven pounds, managed to survive three rounds but couldn't answer the bell for the fourth.**

"The crowd roared and kept roaring," wrote Lardner. "Never had a champion taken such a thorough beating, and never had such a dynamic, merciless hitter been seen. The beauty of Dempsey was that he never let his man recover. He had fought too many miners, cowhands, wranglers, ramrods, brakemen, railroad guards and the like, in saloons, and out, to give his man a chance to recover once he was vulnerable."

The legend of Dempsey was now in motion. Yet, it was far from complete. The Manassa Mauler would defend his title five times and, in the process, become a part of sports history. He knocked out tough Billy Miske in three, and rugged Bill Brennan in twelve. He and French national hero Georges Carpentier combined to build the first million dollar gate in 1921, and Dempsey flattened the courageous Frenchman in four rounds. Jack then coasted to a fifteen-round decision over Tommy Gibbons in 1923 and defended against the Wild Bull of the Pampas, Luis Firpo, on September 14, 1923, in boxing's second million dollar attraction. It was a fight that will live in the memories of men as long as boxing exists.

Over 82,000 fight fans crowded into New York's Polo Grounds to see Dempsey defend against the six foot three, 220-pounder from Argentina. Dempsey, at his 188 pounds, was anything but an imposing figure next to the rugged South American. In fact, according to one version, "Dempsey looked boyish and slight beside Firpo" and the Wild Bull could hit. Dempsey said in his autobiography that every blow Firpo landed staggered him. He even admitted that Firpo came within a hair's breadth of taking the title from him.

Dempsey charged at the opening bell, and was quickly dropped to his knees by a right hand from Firpo. The crowd roared to its feet at the sight of Dempsey on the canvas, and remained on its feet the remainder of the fight. Dempsey leaped up immediately and tore after Firpo, landing two left hooks that dropped Firpo. The Wild Bull was up immediately, but was smacked down again . . . and again . . . and again. Incredibly, Firpo was knocked down seven times in the first round alone. But near the end of the round he lashed out in desperation with a right hand that sent Dempsey flying through the ropes and into the row of reporters at ringside. Dazed, Dempsey half crawled and was half pushed back into the ring, where Firpo, also dazed, tried to finish him off. The bell sounded, ending one of the most exciting rounds in boxing history. It looked to many like Dempsey was through as the second round began, but they hadn't taken his great fighting heart into account. Another ferocious hook dropped Firpo, and he regained his feet only to be knocked down again . . . his ninth trip to the canvas. Once more he rose, and once again Dempsey chopped him down, this time for good. In less than two full rounds, there had been a total of twelve knockdowns, including one that sent the champion of the world out of the ring.

In 1950, twenty-seven years after the fight, writers of the Associated Press voted the fight the most dramatic sporting event of the first half of the century. They also voted Dempsey's victory over Willard one of the ten biggest upsets in sports history.

But the Associated Press also ranked Dempsey's loss to Gene Tunney the second biggest upset ever.

Dempsey's loss of the title he had held for over seven years was a shock to millions of sports fans, but it probably shouldn't have been. After the Firpo fight, Dempsey, for a variety of reasons, took three years off. He became a celebrity of the first rank, hobnobbing with such Hollywood film

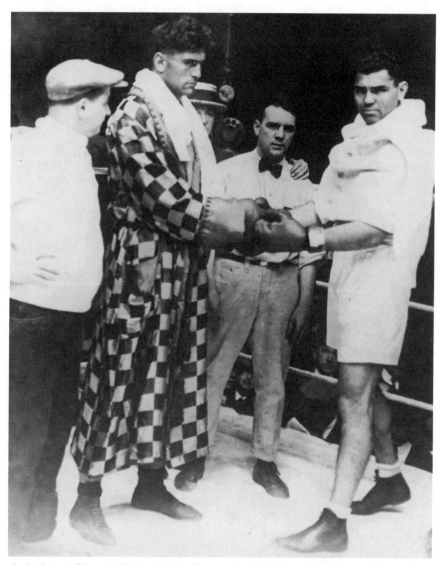

**Luis Angel Firpo (left) and Jack Dempsey shake hands before what will become the single most exciting fight in boxing history. Firpo, challenging for Dempsey's heavyweight title, was dropped seven times in the opening round, but still managed to knock the feared Manassa Mauler completely out of the ring in the first round. The fight took place in 1923, and was won by Dempsey with a knockout in the second round.**

stars as Tom Mix, Douglas Fairbanks and Charlie Chaplin. When he climbed into a Philadelphia ring on September 23, 1926, to face the young and hungry Gene Tunney, he was no longer the Manassa Mauler of old. He lost a ten-round decision, and lost it badly. The public clamored for a rematch and Dempsey took a preliminary bout with rough and ready Jack Sharkey, who was destined to become the heavyweight champ five years later, in 1932. Sharkey was actually outboxing Dempsey when the latter knocked him out in the seventh round. That set the stage for a rematch with Tunney, and one of the most controversial moments in sports history.

Tunney, far ahead on all scorecards, was apparently coasting to another lop-sided victory when Dempsey trapped him with a flurry of punches in the seventh round. Tunney sagged to the canvas, with Dempsey hovering over him. Referee Dave Barry forced Dempsey to a neutral corner, in accordance with the rules, before he started his count over Tunney. Tunney had, at the minimum, fourteen seconds, and maybe even a few more, before he had to rise. When he did, he backpedaled his way to safety. By the next round, he was in full control again, and he finished strongly to easily retain his title.

The fight, however, has become known as "The Long Count," and still haunts Dempsey fans, who claim Tunney could not have made it up in the regular ten seconds.

For all practical purposes, the Dempsey career was over. He did return to the ring from time to time for "grudge" bouts or matches with wrestlers wearing gloves, and he scored knockouts each time. But the official Dempsey score sheet was in after the second Tunney fight, and it looked like this: eighty total bouts, with 49 knockouts, including an amazing 26 in the first round. Dempsey lost seven times, but was only stopped once, that coming at the hands of Fireman Jim Flynn. Dempsey kayoed Flynn in one round in the rematch.

After losing to Tunney, Dempsey's popularity soared to even greater heights. He became "the people's champion"—one of the most popular sports heroes of any day or age.

When George Barton, sports editor of the *Minneapolis Tribune*, was paying tribute to wrestling great Frank Gotch, he wrote that Gotch was "gifted with the personality and friendliness like that which has made Jack Dempsey the most popular sports figure of all time." Sharkey, the only man to ever fight both Joe Louis and Dempsey, captured the exact opposite side of Dempsey when he said, "If Joe Louis and Jack Dempsey ever fought in a telephone booth, I'd bet every dime that I have that it would be Dempsey who would walk out."

The question arises: How could Dempsey be two such completely different people? The answer is "fear," and the way Dempsey reacted to it.

"When I climbed into the ring and looked across at him (Willard), I damned near fainted," Dempsey said years later. "He looked so tremendous. I looked up at Willard and felt scared. Scared enough to have grabbed my robe and run out of the ring—if I dared."

But it all changed, he said, when the bell sounded. Then his fighting instincts took over. After they shook hands, Dempsey entered another world: "As Willard moved away I realized I wasn't just fighting for a title, I was fighting for my life."

It was that response which gave Dempsey the mental edge in his match with Willard and later with Firpo. Dempsey was at his supreme best not against "normal" men like Tunney, but against giants like Fulton, Morris, Willard, and Firpo. It was this type of man that aroused a feeling of fear in Dempsey that caused him to unleash the giant killer that resided deep within him. The trick was to use the emotion, rather than to let it use him.

"Whatever the source of the fear, there is always both a physical and an emotional component to it," wrote David R. Kauss in his book, *Peak Performance*. "Your body is built to respond almost immediately in emergencies, and this 'fight or flight' reaction is provoked by a rush of adrenalin that activates your entire body. Obviously, this can be an excellent source of arousal, but the problems of dealing with the negative aspects of the fear arise equally quickly and dramatically.

"The key," continued Kauss, "is control. If you are able to create a fear that you can also control . . . then it can be a plus."

Dempsey fought out of fear much of his life. In the early days, when he was a skinny kid engaged in "meal money fights" in the mining towns, it was the fear of starvation that made him fight like a madman, or a savage. Later, when he was knocking out the top contenders in the pro ranks, it was the fear of humiliation or physical harm at the hands of much larger men.

When at last Dempsey became content, and the fear left him, so did much of the savagery that had made him so formidable. If Tunney had been fighting the Dempsey of eight years earlier, there is considerable doubt that he could have won. It was not that Tunney wasn't great; he most certainly was. It's more as one writer wrote, in 1919, after the Willard massacre: "On this given day," wrote the jounalist, "no man who ever lived could have stood up to Dempsey."

The hundreds of ring wars (the record books include only 80 official Dempsey fights, but it is generally accepted he fought many, many more, and those records are lost forever) calmed the savage beast that dwelled deep inside Dempsey. What eventually surfaced was the gentle, affable, extremely personable side of Jack Dempsey. After retirement, he opened one of the finest restaurants in New York City, and for many years greeted everyone, friend and stranger, graciously and with open arms.

But the savage beast could return when the fear reappeared. While in his seventies, Dempsey was sitting in a taxicab in New York City when two young men raced up to the cab and flung the doors open. The cabbie

A social gathering finds Polly Tunney seated between two former heavyweight boxing champions. On the left is her husband, Gene, and on the right is Jack Dempsey. Tunney and Dempsey fought twice, but remained friends until Tunney's death in 1978.

was frozen with terror, but not Dempsey. He threw two punches—a right cross and the famed left hook, the same one that had destroyed Willard—and both of the young toughs hit the ground, one after the other. They, too, had been done in by the fear that Dempsey could control as no one ever has, before or since.

Long-time referee Harry Kessler summed up Dempsey's ring style perfectly in an article in *The Sporting News* in 1983: "At his peak, Dempsey was a fantastic fighter, a devastating puncher, always attacking, coming at you from every direction. Anything you left exposed, he would get. Dempsey could take a man out with a single blow or a flurry. He was a killer."

But only inside the ring, or when aroused. Otherwise, he was one of the gentlest champions sports has ever known.

**Gene Tunney, The Fighting Marine, strikes a pose during the early days of his professional career. Tunney won the American light heavyweight championship in 1922, four years before winning the world heavyweight title.**

# GENE TUNNEY

# The Master Planner

In all certainty, there was never a more unlikely world boxing heavyweight champion than James Joseph Tunney, the man they called "The Fighting Marine." Nor has any heavyweight champion been more underrated. Through the years, as discussions of the great heavyweights have arisen, Gene Tunney's name is seldom mentioned. Once in a while he appears in someone's top ten, but he seldom moves higher on the list. Yet, Tunney's record is one of the very best ever compiled. He fought seventy-seven times as a professional and lost just once. He was beaten badly by the Pittsburgh Windmill, Harry Greb, who was one of the toughest—and in the opinion of many, dirtiest—fighters of all time. But Tunney avenged that defeat twice. In addition, Tunney is one of just four heavyweight champions never to have suffered a knockout in his entire career, assuming that Larry Holmes finishes on his feet.

Tunney could box with anyone; as a ring technician he was in the same class as Gentleman Jim Corbett and Muhammad Ali, though he was much smaller, and not as quick as Ali. And Tunney had power, too. He scored forty-two knockouts in his seventy-seven bouts.

Tunney was never an extremely popular champion and for two reasons. First, he was not only the man who took the title from the incredibly popular Jack Dempsey, but he defeated Dempsey in a return match which was marred by controversy. Secondly, Tunney had the affrontery to be an intellectual. He was, in fact, probably the most intelligent man to ever hold the heavyweight title, and could well be considered one of the three or four most intelligent men to ever take part in the gruelling sport of boxing. While his intellect may have endeared him to certain members of the elite boxing crowd, it made him an outcast—someone different, far too different—for the vast majority of boxing fans. Tunney, it seemed, just didn't fit in. Besides, there were some who found his scientific, methodical approach dull.

"We . . . remember the New York Irishman as an elegant, scientific fighter . . . efficient, unexciting, slick defensively, his dark brown eyes constantly staring into an opponent's face, probing for weakness," reported the magazine *Boxing's Greatest Fighters*. "Tunney could outthink, outguess, outwit—and effectively counter—everyone he fought." There, hidden in the praise, was the oft-heard criticism: "unexciting."

The public felt he didn't pack much of a punch either. The myth that Tunney wasn't a hitter developed early in his career when he had to protect his brittle hands from hitting "too hard." He worked hard at making his fists stronger, however, spending a summer as a lumberjack and undertaking a series of hand exercises. He apparently succeeded to a point; but the real problem was in Tunney's psychological makeup.

Perceiving himself primarily as a defensive boxer, Tunney's "objective was always to win a fight without, if possible, ever being hit," according to Randy Roberts, author of the book *Jack Dempsey*. "He did not care in the least whether he won by a knockout or not. As he later admitted, 'I found no joy in knocking people unconscious or battering their faces. The lust for battle and massacre was missing.' In an age when the most popular fighters were of the hit-and-be-hit variety, Tunney was an artistic boxer, a master of the hit without being hit. So it was not surprising that Tunney was not a very popular fighter."

Tunney may not have been the most popular fighter around, but he was the most "thinking" fighter of his era, and maybe ever. He was born into a rather average family in New York's Greenwich Village section in 1898. He received a good education and studied law at New York University before enlisting in the Marine Corps.

As a lad and young man, Tunney was a dreamer, a man who read adventure stories such as *The Three Musketeers* and saw himself in the lead role. He yearned for excitement—to be a hero. His marine division was stationed in France during World War I, but saw no action. It was during this time that Tunney envisioned a fantasy that he would pursue and ultimately force into reality. While sailing down the Rhine River and viewing the impressive castles visible from the deck of his ship, he began dreaming of fighting the world heavyweight boxing champion—not just any heavyweight champ, mind you, but one in particular—Jack Dempsey.

Tunney had boxed in college, mostly as a means of keeping fit. He continued the sport in the service and eventually won recognition as the light heavyweight champion of the forces stationed in Europe. He boxed whenever the opportunity arose, or whenever boredom set in. He learned from the school of hard knocks, but learned effectively. In time he became a highly skilled craftsman, and continually kept his longrange objective—Dempsey—fresh in his mind.

# The New York Times.

"All the News That's Fit to Print."

THE WEATHER

VOL. LXXVI....No. 25,080.     NEW YORK, FRIDAY, SEPTEMBER 24, 1926.     TWO CENTS

# TUNNEY WINS CHAMPIONSHIP, BEATS DEMPSEY IN 10 ROUNDS;
# OUTFIGHTS RIVAL ALL THE WAY, DECISION NEVER IN DOUBT;
# 135,000 PAY MORE THAN $2,000,000 TO SEE BOUT IN THE RAIN

**FLORIDA CONSCRIPTS ALL ITS UNEMPLOYED, CLEAR WRECKAGE**

Militia and Legion Round Up Men in Streets and Set Them to Work.

CALL ISSUED FOR LABORERS

Wants 25,000 Men and Hollywood and Fort Lauderdale 2,000 Each.

LOSS PUT AT $165,000,000.

Dead Now 365, With 1,100 Injured, 500 Seriously—Fight on Disease Goes On.

**North Carolinians Weave Homespun Suit for Walker**

**CROWD ARRIVES SMOOTHLY**

Throngs Ushered Into Philadelphia Stadium Without Confusion.

MANY NOTABLES ATTEND

Governors of Six States and Mayor Walker Among Long List of Officials.

OVER 75,000 FROM HERE

Trains Alone Carry That Number and Others Make the Trip by Automobile.

**GENEVA CONFERENCE ADOPTS COURT PLAN**

Right of Powers to Withdraw Approval of American Reservations Is Recommended.

NEW PROTOCOL NEXT STEP

United States Will Be Invited to Help Draft It—President's Action in Doubt

**Dempsey's Share $850,000; Tunney to Receive $200,000**

**AIRPLANE CARRIES TUNNEY TO SCENE**

Challenger Is First to Make Way to Heavyweight Title Bout Through Air.

RISK DEPLORED BY MANY

Tunney, However, Is Calm Throughout—Calls Flying Least Trying on Nerves.

**TUNNEY ALWAYS MASTER**

Challenger Bewilders His Opponent With His Speed, Accuracy.

AGGRESSIVE IN ALL ROUNDS

Sends Rain of Whiplike Lefts Which Champion Cannot Avoid.

OUTCOME IS A SURPRISE

Dempsey Lacks All Evidence of His Old Aggressiveness—Victor Is Acclaimed.

By JAMES P. DAWSON

**VICTORY IS POPULAR ONE**

Ex-Marine Gets Ovation as He Enters Ring—Crowd 'Boos' Foe.

BIGGEST IN SPORT HISTORY

Rickard's Luck Turns, However, and Distinguished Gathering Is Thoroughly Drenched.

DEMPSEY'S NOSE SUFFERS

Rebuilt for Movies, It Is Target of Challenger as He Piles Up Points for Victory.

By ELMER DAVIS

GENE TUNNEY, THE NEW CHAMPION.

**Champion Tunney Praises the Loser; "I Have No Alibis," Asserts Dempsey**

"He studied the styles of Fitzsimmons, Corbett and Jeffries," wrote Rex Lardner in *The Legendary Champions*. "He read about nerve centers and vulnerable organs in anatomy and kinesiology books. He sharpened his marksmanship in Stillman's Gym in midtown Manhattan. He attended every New York fight Dempsey engaged in, boxed with and quizzed Dempsey's former sparring partners and studied films of Dempsey bouts. It turned out to be a six-year seminar on the psychology, weapons and possible weaknesses of Dempsey."

By most accounts, Tunney was obsessed with Dempsey. Every move he made was with the forethought of fighting, and beating, Dempsey. Once, while playing golf, Tunney ran after his golf ball throwing phantom punches and mumbling the champ's name over and over.

But Dempsey was just part of an overall, grander scheme. Tunney wanted desperately to be someone in life. He longed for the plaudits of higher society, to be recognized and accepted. He yearned for money, fame, security, and, eventually, a wife of stature, breeding and position. Boxing was only the means to an end. While Dempsey fought out of a pent-up rage and a fear of defeat, humiliation and suffering, Tunney fought as a way to lift himself up from the doldrums of day-to-day life. Dempsey, then, fought with a fury, while Tunney fought with a cold calculation, measuring every step, every move, every punch.

Tunney's route to Dempsey was blocked by several tough cookies, including ex-Dempsey victims Georges Carpentier, whom Tunney kay-oed in the 15th round, and Tommy Gibbons, whom he stopped in the 12th. By comparison, Dempsey had taken out Carpentier in four and had to go a full fifteen to earn a decision over the scrappy Gibbons. But the toughest man in Tunney's path was Greb. Tunney had won the American Light Heavyweight Championship on January 13, 1922, with a 12-round decision over Battling Levinsky. Four fights later he ran into Greb and suffered a horrendous beating. Greb bloodied his nose in the first round, broke it in the second, and pummeled him from beginning to end, smashing him in the face with lefts, rights, elbows and head butts. Blood poured from all over Tunney's face; several veteran writers called it the worst beating they had ever seen a man take in the ring. Tunney refused to go down, however, defiantly lasting out the battle. And, while being beaten from corner to corner, he began plotting how he could beat Greb in the rematch.

Boxing Commissioner William Muldoon, a former champion wrestler, was amazed when Tunney showed up in his office the next day, ready for a return match. Muldoon thought that Tunney was way out of his class against Greb, and told him so. Yet Tunney regained his title from Greb with a fifteen-round decision less than a year later in a close fight and then handled him easily in a third match. They tangled twice more in no-decision fights, but the general consensus was that Tunney won both, and rather handily.

Anyone who had ever doubted Tunney's fortitude and intent should have had no problems with either after the second Greb fight. His courage was plain enough for anyone to see, and his intent was to make boxing "his game."

Rice, calling the first Greb fight "perhaps the bloodiest fight I ever covered," reported that "Greb handled Tunney like a butcher hammering a steak. By the third round, Gene was literally wading in his own blood. I saw Gene a few days later. His face looked as though he'd taken the wrong end of a razor fight."

Despite the beating, however, Tunney had great respect for Greb. When Greb died in 1926 after an automobile accident and complications from an eye operation, Tunney served as a pallbearer and spoke glowing words for the fallen warrior.

A string of impressive victories finally gained Tunney his long-awaited shot at Dempsey, but the two fighters' conditions before the climactic battle could hardly have been more opposite. While Tunney was fighting and honing his skills to a razor's edge, Dempsey was mired down in a multitute of personal problems. He and his wife, movie actress Estelle Taylor, were on the verge of a divorce, and his long-time manager, Jack Kearns, was suing him. Dempsey looked flat in camp, and was outboxed by a slick Tommy Loughran, who would eventually become light heavyweight champ of the world.

Dempsey actually entered the ring against Tunney without having defended his title in over three years. It was the longest period the world's heavyweight championship had ever been put on ice. But the fight itself had everything a fan, or promoter, could want. Tex Rickard, who engineered the contest, was delighted with the matchup.

"Dempsey-Tunney had everything," he said. "Boxer versus puncher, youth versus age, and the unknown. How much did Dempsey, after being off three years, have left? I figured the gate would be good."

It was. Fans came from all over the globe. Politicians—including the governors from six states—movie actors, European royalty and high society were there. Philadelphia was wall-to-wall people for days leading up to the fight, causing one veteran writer to say he had never seen anything like it, and doubted he ever would again. Despite rain, over 120,000 people—the largest crowd ever to see a boxing match— showed up at Susquicentennial Stadium, and paid a record $1,895,733, an amazing figure for 1927. What they saw was a beautiful tactical fight by Tunney, one that unmasked the legendary Dempsey and left him, in his own words, "an old man."

Tunney almost always mapped out a particular stategy for a fight and then stuck to it. Originally, he had planned to fight Gibbons at long range, but he switched to an inside fight plan after studying Gibbons closely. It was the perfect way to handle him, and it shocked not only Gibbons, but the crowd of some 40,000. Tunney dismantled Gibbons, and he dismantled Dempsey.

**31**

**Gene Tunney (facing the camera) prepares to throw a right hand at Jack Dempsey during their championship fight September 22, 1927, in Chicago. Tunney retained his title with a 10-round decision.**

He entered the Dempsey fight with a "secret weapon." He had observed that the Manassa Mauler was susceptible to a straight right when thrown with precision and accuracy at precisely the right moment. He perfected the move in his training camp, and waited patiently for his opportunity. It came early in the first round; Dempsey missed with a left hook, and Tunney countered with a thunderous right hand that lit high on the champion's cheek. Tunney called it the hardest punch he ever threw, and Dempsey admitted that it hurt him badly. But more than that, it demoralized him. Dempsey had to clinch to last the round, and when he sat down in his corner he knew he was in for a long, long night. Tunney, calm and poised, boxing like a machine, hammered away at the legend for ten rounds, and won a unanimous decision. After the fight, both men displayed considerable sportsmanship. Dempsey demanded that a cornerman lead him to the new champ (Dempsey's left eye was swollen shut, there was a cut over the right, and he could barely move his legs) and congratulated him. Tunney, in his characteristic manner, told Dempsey he "would always be the champ."

But the affection between the two disintegrated before the second fight, which came September 22, 1927, in Chicago's Soldier Field. A crowd of 104,943—which, again, included many of the nation's most colorful and influential people—paid an astounding $2,658,660, the all-time record for a live gate.

"A carnival spirit prevailed in Chicago," wrote one journalist. "Crowds were so dense in the Loop that it was impossible to make any headway on the sidewalks. Hotel lobbies and rooms were jammed. Special trains rolled in from every city in the country, with section after section added as the cars neared their destination. Daredevils flew in by plane from Michigan and New York. Hour after hour, celebrities detrained at the heavily thronged depot . . ."

What the fans saw was pretty much a repeat of the Philadelphia bout- except for a few seconds in the seventh round. In that short time span, the most controversial moment in sports history took place. It was to be relived, debated and fought over for decades, and will never be settled to the satisfaction of everyone.

Tunney had the fight under control for the first six rounds. Dempsey, in his autobiography, said "I never should have stepped into the ring that night. From the beginning, Gene Tunney held the advantage, though I was grimly determined to win back my title. He had me staggering and leaning against the ropes by the second round. By the third and fourth rounds, I was in a bad way, weary and bleeding. I felt flat-footed and I found I was having difficulty breathing. But I wouldn't give up for anything."

And then it happened. Dempsey charged Tunney and caught him with a powerful right, followed by a left hook and several more lesser blows. Tunney, for the first time in his career, crumpled to the floor, grasping for the lower ring strand, one leg buckled beneath him.

**In an uncharacteristic pose, world heavyweight champion Gene Tunney displays his back and shoulder muscles. Tunney, rather a recluse who shied away from publicity, was perhaps the most intelligent fighter of his generation. He engaged in a total of 77 bouts, and lost just once. He is one of four heavyweight champions to have never been knocked out during his entire career.**

The controversy arose when Dempsey refused to go to a neutral corner, as specified in the new rules. When referee Dave Barry pointed for him to leave, Dempsey refused. "I wanted him to get up so I could kill the son of a bitch," Dempsey was later quoted as saying. But Barry insisted he go to the neutral corner, and walked him to it; then he returned to Tunney, starting the count at one. By nine, Tunney was back on his feet. Then he backpedaled to safety. The frustrated Dempsey chased him futilely, and once yelled at the champ to come and fight, but Tunney was too poised for that. He wouldn't fight again until he was in complete control of his faculties.

Tunney survived the round, decked Dempsey for a second in the eighth, and won going away. The controversy raged for weeks, however, and many felt Dempsey had won, as Tunney had been on the canvas for a total of fourteen seconds, minimum.

Through the years, Dempsey and Tunney have offered varying opinions on the subject of Tunney's ability to rise.

**34**

Tunney had pulled off the near impossible—twice. He had met the savage beast and had prevailed. Of course, everyone admitted that the Dempsey Tunney fought in 1926 and 1927 was a far cry from the lean, hungry Dempsey who battered the huge Jess Willard into submission in 1919.

Tunney achieved the miraculous primarily because of two factors. The first was his obsession and long-range planning and the ability he had to assess an opponent and do exactly what was demanded to insure victory. But there was another reason, too:

"One night at the beginning of my long training period I awakened suddenly and felt my bed shaking," said Tunney. "It seemed fantastic. Ghosts or what? Then I understood. It was I who was shaking, trembling so hard that I made the bed tremble. I was that much afraid—afraid of what Dempsey would do to me. The fear was lurking in the back of my mind and set me quaking in my sleep, the nightmare thought of myself being beaten down by Dempsey's shattering punches. The vision was of myself, bleeding, mauled and helpless, sinking to the canvas and being counted out. I couldn't stop trembling."

But he found solace and refuge, he said, in prayer. And in his ironwilled discipline. As a young man Tunney devised innumerable games—such as standing on a chair and counting to 500 when dog tired, just to make himself overcome the temptation to lie down—and that training came back to fortify him in his moment of apprehension.

"I simply had to close the doors of my mind to destructive thought and divert my thinking to other things," he said. "It took discipline. And, again, prayer and faith were pillars of strength to me."

Grantland Rice saw Tunney's secret as concentration—dedication to a single-minded pursuit: ". . . I can read the figure of a man who dedicated himself to a task as no other athlete, with the exception of Ben Hogan, ever dedicated himself," wrote Rice, before the dawn of two other athletes (Rocky Marciano and Dan Gable) who would fit the same mold. "For at least six years, the Tunney of Philadelphia fame trained for that first big chance as perfectly as a man can train: no drinking, no smoking, proper food, proper exercise, no deviation from the straight and narrow, all harnessed to a tremendous power of concentration."

Tunney fought just once after Dempsey, outclassing Tom Heeney in twelve rounds. Then Tunney retired to a life of scholarly and financial pursuits. He was independently wealthy—having earned a cool $990,000 from the second Dempsey fight alone—and was a pillar of society, sought out by celebrities, politicians and the status conscious. He married Polly Lauder, an heiress who was related to the fabulous Carnegies, and moved into private business, where he became very successful. His son, John, eventually became a United States Congressman from California.

At the peak of his career, Gene Tunney was fit and trim and handsome. Tunney engaged in 77 professional fights, and lost just once . . . to Harry Greb in 1922.

As the years passed, Dempsey and Tunney became fast friends and were often seen in one another's company. Dempsey campaigned on behalf of John Tunney, and was shattered when word of Tunney's death reached him on December 7, 1978. He had cried the night Tunney took his title from him, and he cried the night he heard his greatest adversary, and true friend, had died. Tunney was eighty-one when death claimed him.

Angelo Dundee, the trainer of Muhammad Ali, labelled Tunney one of the most underrated champions of all time. Of that there can be little doubt. He has never received his due, and is largely a forgotten fighter. Even his own son was surprised when he found out that the famed martial arts star, Bruce Lee, had read and studied his father's book on his boxing career.

"Bruce and I were having dinner with Senator John Tunney," wrote Linda Lee. "Now, not many people of Bruce's generation knew that Gene Tunney had written a couple of books after he retired as undefeated heavyweight champion and Senator Tunney was flabbergasted. . . ."

"Gene Tunney brought a new look to boxing," wrote Lardner. "The passing of the crown to Tunney reflects a turning point in American culture. Dempsey's determination and brute force were frontier virtues. Tunney was a disciplined student whose aspirations went beyond the ring."

Prolific reader, student of Shakespeare, social climber, a man of great intellect, Tunney was a different breed of boxer. He really wasn't a fighter in the true sense, yet he competed successfully with the greatest fighters of his era—legendary men like Dempsey, Greb and Gibbons—and defeated them. His achievements are a remarkable testimonial to the qualities of determination, perseverance, poise and dedication.

Yet in the final evaluation it may have been Tunney's ability to build a master plan—no matter how far-fetched it seemed—and stick to it at all costs, that led him to the top of the pugilistic world. In that respect Tunney stands supreme in athletic history.

**World heavyweight boxing champion Rocky Marciano sports a big grin after finishing a workout. Marciano had plenty to smile about when he retired from boxing in 1956—he compiled a record of 49-0, which included 43 knockouts.**

# ROCKY MARCIANO

## Champion Without Fear

Fear is one of the most basic responses to the human condition. It is virtually impossible to imagine a time when the creature we know as man existed without fear, a constant companion poised to whisper its message of intimidation and confinement. There are various types of fear, to be sure, but perhaps the most basic is that which accompanies the prospect of physical harm or injury. Prehistoric man had to contend with fear on a day-to-day basis as he ventured out into a hostile world, confronting huge and terrifying carnivores in his never-ending search for food.

While all homo sapiens encounter fear at some level, there are some special, very rare individuals who seldom experience fear's immobilizing embrace. These people are, for reasons not yet totally understood by scientists, largely immune to fear. And this is a fact that we, as a species, can be thankful for.

"It is plain that society needs such people," wrote David T. Lykken, professor of psychiatry and psychology at the University of Minnesota, in the September 1982 edition of *Psychology Today*. "Were it not for the fact that a small percentage of every generation has this quality of relative fearlessness, we would not have advanced this far as a species."

It takes little imagination to suppose where we would be today without the incredible initiative and courage demonstrated by such amazing men as Christopher Columbus, Hernando DeSoto, Jim Bridger and the like. Consider the staggering courage, or lack of fear, exhibited by Columbus and his men as they set out in 1492 in a sailing ship little bigger than a modern house, ready to brave the great and dreaded unknown we now call the Atlantic Ocean.

"A small minority in every generation is relatively fearless," continued Lykken. "From their ranks come many of our astronauts, our Medal of Honor winners, our most audacious leaders."

And from those same ranks have come some of the greatest prizefighters.

It takes vast amounts of courage to crawl into a ring and fight. Boxing is one of the very few sports where the object is not only to score points, but to hurt the other man. Boxing purists may argue that the true art is the science; that the beauty is not in knocking the foe senseless, but in outpointing him. That may be well and good, but it is deceiving, because you can outbox your foe for nine rounds of a ten-round bout and then get kayoed in the tenth, and lose. One must conclude, then, that the object is really to score a knockout; that is the only way to assure victory. The knockout is therefore the ultimate goal.

Thousands of men have climbed into a prize ring in search of fame and fortune, but few have been as successful as Rocky Marciano. In fact, no other heavyweight champion—into the 1980s —had ever completed his entire professional career undefeated. Marciano, nicknamed the Brockton Blockbuster, fought forty-nine times as a professional, and scored forty-nine wins. Only five of his opponents went the distance, with the amazing Ted Lowry earning that distinction twice.

In the record book, Marciano stands triumphantly alone at the top of the heap. Much of the credit must be given to his ferocious dedication and his non-stop style of fighting; he was a buzzsaw, a gattling gun of flying leather. He never took a backward step, never gave a foe a moment's rest. He asked no quarter and gave none. Rocky Marciano came to fight.

But while his physical performance was awe-inspiring and intimidating, so was his mental performance. Marciano had the mental edge over all of his opponents because Marciano was a man who knew no fear. His lack of fear catapulted him to the very uppermost pinnacle of the sports world, and perhaps played a role in his premature death at the age of forty-six in an Iowa cornfield.

As a boxer, Marciano was a late bloomer. He had engaged in a few street fights in his youth and a couple of boxing matches while in the army, but he had his heart set on becoming a major league baseball player. He and several of his childhood friends managed tryouts with the Chicago Cubs, Marciano hoping to make the grade as a catcher. Their dreams were short-lived, however, and they returned to their hometown of Brockton, Massachussets, with little hope for the future.

But Marciano, desperate to escape the drudgery of a lifetime of work in the shoe factories in which his father had toiled for years, began fighting professionally, just to earn money. At first he was clumsy and awkward, and attracted little attention. But Marciano had two overwhelming factors in his favor: he could hit with unbelievable power, and he was utterly fearless.

A middleweight, Arthur Thayer, said that Marciano had ice water in his veins. He could actually sleep before a match—any match. And a fighter's record meant nothing to him. In just his fourth professional bout, he was matched against a young slugger named Bobby Quinn. Marciano's trainer then, Allie Columbo, didn't want the match because Quinn already had fourteen knockouts to his credit. Marciano insisted. "Take the fight," he is quoted as saying by Everett M. Skehen, in his superb biography, *Marciano.* "What do we care about Quinn?"

"Columbo was tense, pacing around the house as if Rocky were going into a championship fight. Not Rocky, though. He took his usual two-hour nap, and then had a rare steak."

Marciano flattened Quinn in three rounds. It was his fifth straight knockout, and he followed it up with eleven in a row more before Don Mogard managed to last ten rounds on May 23, 1949. The Quinn fight was similar to many others not only in its abrupt ending, but in Marciano's disposition. While most fighters are a bundle of nervous energy before entering the ring, Marciano had to struggle to stay awake. He was simply unafraid.

One of the finest examples of the Marciano courage came October 26, 1951, in New York's Madison Square Garden. The young Marciano was pitted against Joe Louis, the famed Brown Bomber who had been heavyweight champion of the world for twelve years. Though Louis was on a comeback trail after retirement and was well past his prime, he had two factors in his favor: he still had tremendous power in his fists, and he had a reputation that could chill most opponents.

As Skehan points out, Louis, in his prime, ". . . had become a fighting machine that always moved forward and seemed indestructible. He forced his opponents to fight defensively, and many of them were paralyzed by fear long before they entered the ring.

"But Marciano was fearless. No fighter could stalk him, because he was a brawler always on the offense. He had kayoed 32 of 37 opponents and had never been defeated as a professional. He was very confident of a victory over Louis.

" 'Are your worried?' a reporter asked Rocky.

" 'No. I'm not worried,' Rocky said. 'It's just another fight.'

" 'Do you think you'll win?'

" 'Win?' Rocky said. 'Yeah, I think I'll win.'

" 'That was a dumb question the reporter asked today,' Rocky told Columbo when they were alone that night. 'If I didn't think I was going to win, why the hell would I be fighting?' "

It was, however, an honest question by the reporter; he undoubtedly felt a man of Marciano's still slight reputation should be intimidated by the prospect of facing the legendary Louis. Marciano did carry a healthy respect for Louis, but he did not fear him in the least. Fear was foreign to Marciano; it never visited him, in the ring or out. He constantly talked friends into undertaking dangerous adventures with him, whether it involved risky business ventures in far-off places like Cuba, or airplane rides in the dead of night under adverse conditions.

Once, while riding in an airplane, Rocky's brother, Sonny, and a friend became terrified as a storm began slamming the plane around like the ball in a pinball machine. Marciano was fast asleep, and finally his brother, frightened beyond restraint, could stand it no longer. He awoke Rocky.

" 'Hey Rock,' Sonny said. 'This doesn't look good. Maybe we're gonna crash or something.'[1]

" 'Is that all you're waking me up for?' Rocky said. 'What's the matter with you? What are you worried about? If it's your time, it's your time and there's nothing you can do about it. If it isn't, then there's nothing to worry about.' " And Marciano—Rocky, that is—fell back asleep while his brother and friend continued to fret and stew.

Little wonder that a fight in a ring, against a man even of the caliber of Joe Louis, could not arouse fear in Marciano. Though he was outweighed 212 pounds to 187 by Louis and was shy nearly four inches in height, Marciano hammered Louis viciously before knocking him out in the eighth round.

"Marciano would keep coming, keep coming and never back up," said longtime boxing official Harry Kessler in a 1983 article in *Sporting News*. "He'd throw punches for 180 seconds each round and any one of them could knock a man out. Marciano was impossible to discourage, and he was absolutely fearless. Pain wasn't even in his vocabulary. He'd take four punches to land one, but that one was the equivalent of four from someone else."

Perhaps no fight underscored Marciano's courage and his willingness to trade punches more dramatically than his brutal confrontation with Carmen Vingo on December 30, 1949. Marciano entered with a 24-0 record, while Vingo was 27-3 and known for his big punch and even bigger heart. For four rounds they stood toe-to-toe, the six-foot-four Vingo staggering the shorter, constantly-charging Marciano on several occasions, while Rocky dumped Vingo twice. Vingo hurt Marciano badly in the fifth, but the Brockton Blockbuster fought back even harder and, in the sixth, sent Vingo crashing to the canvas with a left hook to the head. Vingo was finished before he hit, but when he landed his head snapped back and slammed hard against the floor. Minutes later, he went into a coma. He was taken to a hospital and the last rites of the Catholic Church were administered at one point. Vingo recovered, but he never fought again.

---

[1]Excerpts from the book *Rocky Marciano: Biography of a First Son*, by Everett Skehan. Copyright 1977 by Everett M. Skehan. Reprinted by permission of Houghton Mifflin Company.

The rest of his career, Marciano had to conquer the fear of seriously injuring—or even killing—a man with his fists.

The ultimate tribute to Marciano's greatest asset came in the October 1972 issue of *Ring* magazine, when Nat Fleischer, the world's number one expert on boxing, ranked Rocky the "most courageous" fighter of all time.

Marciano's lack of fear may have had two origins. First, there is the genetic strain. It is the quality determined by one's ancestors, passed on by one's parents. Lykken suggests that this characteristic, this license for bravado acts, ". . . can only be found in the personality trait of fearfulness —or, as I call it, 'fear IQ.' People high in this trait avoid risk and stress and strong stimulation; people at the low end, those endowed with a low fear IQ, are the group from which we get our adventures, our explorers, our astronauts, often our leaders."

But Marciano also developed his lack of fear through rigorous physical training. It is thought by some that Marciano was the most superbly conditioned heavyweight boxer of all time. He was obsessed with conditioning, and his training was a labor of love.

Early in his amateur days, Rocky was disqualified in a fight for kicking his opponent in the groin. It happened when Marciano, out of shape for lack of training, was being embarrassed by a slick opponent. Rather than accept defeat, he lashed out a foot in frustration. Though disqualified, he was able to rationalize the defeat because the other man had not beaten him with his fists, but with the rules. Nevertheless, Marciano was humiliated by the experience, and vowed never to fight again unless he was totally prepared. He kept that vow until the end of his career.

Marciano became addicted to exercise.

"His extraordinary fortitude was part courage and part physical condition," wrote Red Smith, the most respected of all sports journalists. "Even in the months when he had no fight in sight, Rocky would train, living in the airport cottage above Grossinger's in the Catskills, jogging, hiking, sparring, punching the bag, skipping rope, doing calisthenics.

"Rocky Marciano couldn't box like Tunney and probably couldn't hit like Louis, but in one respect he had no challenger. He was the toughest, strongest most completely dedicated fighter who ever wore gloves.

"Fear wasn't in his vocabulary and pain had no meaning."

"That great desire to win was so evident in the guy," said Angelo Dundee, Ali's trainer. "I could see it right from the beginning. In my opinion, Marciano was the most underrated heavyweight of all time. He had so much more than they ever gave him credit for. He was capable of getting those bigger, heavier guys and destroying them."

Marciano liked to experiment with various conditioning techniques. He trained secretly as a young boy to develop his strength, went on long, long walks (twenty miles a day, sometimes) to increase his stamina, and threw

**Rocky Marciano, one of the most relaxed and fearless fighters of all time, smiles while standing on the scales prior to his challenge of champion Jersey Joe Walcott (at his side) in 1952. Marciano weighed in at 184 pounds, while Walcott was 196 pounds.**

punches in long flurries while up to his shoulders in water, forcing his ham-like fists through the resistance of the water until his shoulders burned with the exertion. He had absolute, total confidence in his ability to outlast his foe, no matter whom it might be. It was that confidence, based on the preparation of the physical labor, that gave him the mental edge in the actual competition.

Marcel Cerdan, one of boxing's greatest middleweight champions (before he was killed in a plane crash in 1949 en route to New York to fight Jake LaMotta) recognized Marciano's greatest asset when the Rock was still an unknown.

" 'He don't know how to fight, but his heart, she's so big, she does not believe in defeat,' Cerdan told Colombo. 'He'll fight anybody, and he bleed and bleed and bleed, but always he come back.' "

During his climb to the top, Marciano's life became more and more dominated by his sport. Boxing was all he thought about, all that mattered. Even his family—which then consisted of his wife Barbara and infant daughter—had to take a back seat.

"Marciano's preoccupation with physical conditioning cannot be overstressed," wrote Skehan. "He was eager to train every day before a fight, and, unlike most heavyweights, he sometimes went to camp months before there was even a fight scheduled for him.

"Even Joe Frazier, the former champion who prided himself on being fit, a slugger who, like Marciano, relied heavily on stamina and strength to bull his way through the defenses of an opponent, did not train with anywhere near the same dedication that Marciano devoted to it.

" 'I've been to camp eight weeks,' Frazier said before his title bout with Muhammad Ali in Manila (September, 1975). 'The longest in my life, and I feel I'm ready.'

"It is safe to speculate that eight weeks of training would not have satisfied Marciano had he been scheduled to fight Ali. He had often trained for four or five months to go against far less skilled opponents. For he truly believed that there was something about long-distance training that increased a man's endurance, just as a slow, sensible diet trims off the fat more evenly than a dramatic crash program. And, although no one can ever be certain, there is reason to doubt whether Ali or any fighter could have worn Marciano down and destroyed his defenses the way Muhammad did to Foreman and Frazier."

Marciano's fearlessness was a combination of a gift and his own drive and zeal; while he was born with a spirit that rebelled at the thought of shrinking from danger, he also nurtured that spirit by his own irrepressible desire. Losing was so foreign to him, in concept, that he had no fear of it. When he continued to win, often with ease, his confidence reached a point of no return. He would never fear to do battle with any man, anywhere.

In the summer of 1952, Marciano was on the trail of heavyweight champion Jersey Joe Walcott. He was ready for the ultimate challenge, and he knew it.

"He came to Grossinger's (a top New York City gym) lean and hungry, obsessed with but a single purpose of mind and spirit—to become heavyweight champion of the world. Mesmerized by the magniloquence of his personal crusade, he retreated from the world, carrying in the inner

**Challenger Rocky Marciano (left) applies the pressure to champion Jersey Joe Walcott during their heavyweight title fight September 23, 1952, in Philadelphia. Trailing throughout most of the fight, Marciano rallied to knock Walcott cold in the thirteenth round and become the new heavyweight boxing champion of the world. (Wide World Photos)**

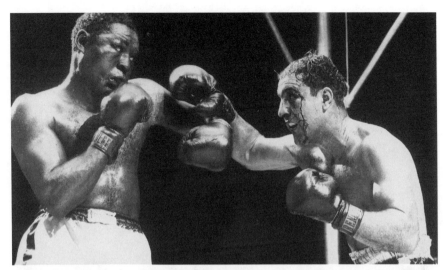

**With blood streaming down his face, heavyweight boxing champion Rocky Marciano pursues challenger Ezzard Charles during their 1954 title fight in New York. Marciano and Charles, who was world champion earlier, fought twice, with Marciano taking a 15-round decision in the first go-around, and stopping Charles in the eighth round the second time. (Wide World Photos)**

sanctums of his soul a reverence and dedication equal in magnitude, if not motivation, to the religious zeal of a Trappist Monk," said Skehen.

"It's curious, but understandable, how the great athletes of any sport never allow themselves to consider the possibility of defeat. Ted Williams expected to get a hit whenever he went to the plate. Jack Nicklaus is convinced he can win any golf tournament he enters. And Marciano was the same way, always certain that he would win. Defeat was an ugly specter, made to remain invisible somewhere in the shady caverns of the fighter's subconscious. He was as convinced as any man could ever be of his own infallability. It was one of his most important assets."

Marciano won the title September 23, 1952, when he knocked out Walcott in the thirteenth round. Marciano was trailing on all scorecards and bleeding profusely when he slammed a crushing right hand against the jaw of the slick, but aging champion. Walcott slumped to the floor, dead to the world, and Rocky was the king of boxing.

He defended his title just six times, and retired undefeated in April of 1956. His last defense was a ninth-round knockout of light-heavyweight champion Archie Moore on September 21, 1955.

Marciano was in constant demand around the world, and spent his retirement flying from spot to spot, visiting old friends and making new ones. He was an amiable, friendly man, though extremely tight with a buck, even to the point of paranoia. His end was tragic, because it was so

Rocky Marciano (right), several years after his retirement from boxing, shakes hands with a young heavyweight named Dan Hodge. Marciano retired with a professional record of 49-0. Hodge, national Golden Gloves heavyweight champion, was also a national champion wrestler.

premature and could have been avoided. It may have been, in part, due to his lack of fear.

Marciano was a fatalist; he didn't fear death because, he said, when it was a fellow's time to go he was going to go, regardless. His philosophy encompassed the belief that it did no good whatever to worry, so he never did.

A private airplane carrying Marciano, a young businessman from Des Moines and the pilot left Midway Airport in Chicago at 5:30 p.m. August 31, 1969, the day before Marciano's forty-sixth birthday. Landing conditions in Des Moines, where the trio was headed, were poor, and the pilot was unqualified to fly under such conditions. One can easily imagine Rocky stating that nothing could happen, and, if it did, it was the way it was supposed to be, anyway.

Maybe he was right about the last point. The pilot contacted the Des Moines airport almost three hours after leaving Chicago, saying he was confused and in need of assistance and direction. Minutes later, the craft slammed into an oak tree in the midst of an Iowa cornfield. The plane was destroyed and all three passengers were killed.

Had Rocky known fear, perhaps he might have instructed the pilot to postpone taking off from Chicago until conditions were more favorable. But that was not Marciano's way.

Trying to explain why the number of fearless people seems so tiny, Lykken wrote that "people with low fear IQ's tend to get killed off before they reproduce." Marciano did have a daughter and son, but he was still killed far before his time.

Rocky Marciano was a hero to millions. Cassius Clay, as a young boy in Louisville, sat by the radio and listened in awe as Marciano's name was screamed to the world as the winner of fight after fight. Those moments helped to mold Clay's own burning desire to be champion of the world, and Clay never forgot Marciano. In his autobiography, Ali relates how he drove at breakneck speed to Marciano's funeral, and tells of his rage at other ring greats for taking the opportunity to sign autographs when they should have been paying their respects to the memory of Marciano.

Marciano loved his sport and, though he was a humble man, took a fierce pride in it and his abilities.

"I enjoyed it (boxing), I liked it," he said in his slow, articulate manner. "I never really knew fear, I never was really hurt. And I just think that in my prime I could have fought with anybody alive."

Through the years, Marciano's message has remained clear. Total dedication to training and condition can enable one to scale the highest mountain. But Marciano left another legacy, too—that of a fighter who was, for whatever reasons, totally devoid of fear.

**The image of Muhammad Ali looms larger than life in the background as a young, aspiring boxer pauses during a workout. Ali, one of the most charismatic champions of all time, is still a hero to millions around the world. (Photo by Greg Mellis)**

# MUHAMMAD ALI

# The Master of Arousal

"One needs one's opponent," wrote James Zabriske in his interesting little book, *The Handbook of Inner Sports.* "It is what the American Indian knew. His enemy, so called, brought out the best in him."

There is a deep and primeval truth in those words. It was true of Achilles meeting Hector, of Gotch meeting Hackenschmidt, of Dempsey meeting Firpo, of Tunney meeting Dempsey.

In the case of Muhammad Ali, it was true threefold. First, there was Sonny Liston; then came Joe Frazier—three times—and then there was George Foreman. They were three of the most formidable heavyweights of all time. On any given night, Liston, Frazier and Foreman could have taken on anyone and had an excellent chance of victory. Ali fought the trio a total of six times, and won five. And, it must be said, he was past his prime on four of those occasions.

How good was Muhammad Ali/Cassius Clay at his best? Forget about the aging Ali that most of us remember after the exile. Oh, that fighter was plenty good, one of the top five or six heavyweights ever. But concentrate on the young Ali, or the man who was 29-0 before the United States government forced a three and one-half year exile on him as a fighter for his failure to permit induction into the armed services. That Ali was a dancing master, faster than any heavyweight ever. A large man at 6-3 and nearly 220 pounds, he possesed a huge heart and an iron chin. *Ring* magazine said his ability to take a punch on the jaw was among the top five in all of boxing history. He wouldn't stay down after Joe Frazier hit him with a devastating left hook in the fifteenth round of their first fight, and he wouldn't quit after Ken Norton broke his jaw in the early going of a twelve rounder.

How good was Ali in his prime? Let Jersey Joe Walcott, the former heavyweight champion of the world, and a man who fought both Joe Louis and Rocky Marciano, tell us:

"Clay could beat Dempsey, Louis, Charles, Marciano and a fellow named Jersey Joe Walcott," said Walcott in a story published in *Ring* magazine in 1963. "Clay is too big and punches too fast and hard and moves too quick for all us oldtimers. This kid has speed in his hands and feet like a welterweight. He puts his punches together better than any heavyweight champ I've ever seen.

"Dempsey and Louis and the rest of us would be too small to beat this big, rangy kid. Clay would just have to stay away from us for a few rounds and then start throwing his combinations."

Walcott, champion in 1951 and '52, added that Clay's skills were deceptive because of his blazing speed. It enabled him to do things, and to get away with maneuvers, that others could not.

Perhaps no other fighter ever beat three men of the caliber of Liston, Frazier and Foreman. And not only did Ali beat them, he stopped all three of them. Liston went a total of eight rounds in two attempts, Frazier couldn't answer the bell for the fifteenth for their battle in Manilla, and Foreman was knocked out, incredibly, in the eighth round in Zaire. In the first fight with Liston, and also against Foreman, Ali was a huge underdog. The upsets were staggering, mind boggling. Ali was able to pull off those wins with his great natural physical talents—and through his amazing mind games. Ali was the master of arousal, a man who could psych the opposition out in a remarkable fashion.

"A person's long-standing personality traits are less relevant to producing good athletic performance than are the individual states of mind, like anxiety or excitement, that the athlete can bring about at particular times for the purpose of readying," writes David R. Kauss in *Peak Performance*.

Allowing oneself to go out of control for brief periods of time is often the key element to successful mental warfare. The technique, known as arousal, was essential to the early success of Clay/Ali, particularly in his stunning success against Liston in 1963.

Only Jack Dempsey, the feared Manassa Mauler of the 1920s, carried a more formidable presence into the prize ring than Liston. Bursting onto the national sports scene in 1959, Liston was an ex-con with an intimidating stare and a pulverizing punch. At 6-1, with 220 pounds of sheer muscle, he was a frightening specter in the ring. A man who seldom smiled, he seemed intent only on busting someone's face wide open with sledgehammer fists.

In 1959 and 1960, Liston scored nine straight knockouts, including impressive victories over high-ranked contenders Cleveland Williams and Zora Foley. Williams, a perfectly-muscled man with a long string of knockouts himself, was avoided by most heavyweights of the era. But Liston rendered him unconscious twice—once in the third round and again in the second. He flattened Foley in just three rounds.

Liston decisioned highly-regarded Eddie Machen in a track meet (Machen running and Liston pursuing) and then scored two more quick kayos. When he climbed into the ring to meet champion Floyd Patterson, it was one of the few times in history that a challenger was favored.

"On the night he faces Patterson, Liston will move out of his corner dead set on annihilation, his eyes filled with evil, his powerful legs conditioned by girlish rope-skipping, his meanness fortified by raw meat," wrote Marsh Smith of *Life* magazine. "Ringside will be no place for the squeamish, the moralistic or the faint of heart. And in the ring it will take all of the champion's courage and skill to survive."

Patterson barely did survive. Liston stopped him in just two minutes and six seconds of the first round. Their rematch seven months later took just four seconds more. Liston was, according to many followers of the sport, one of the most terrifying men ever to climb into a ring, and virtually unbeatable.

"Liston actually is an awesome heavyweight," wrote A.S. Young in his unauthorized biography of Liston in 1963. "People watch him fight or work out and they come away amazed—by his strength and stamina, by his speed and agility, his ring-deadly demeanor. His demolition job on Patterson was so thorough, so swift, so complete that the near nineteen thousand in-person onlookers were simply shocked, stunned, startled into silence. Not even Louis could have beaten Liston's time or thoroughness, Jack Dempsey could not have been more devastating."

Small wonder that virtually no one gave Clay any kind of a chance at all against the ferocious Liston when Sonny chose to give Clay a chance for the title February 25, 1964.

Following the second Patterson fight, Liston's record was an imposing 35-1, with twenty-five knockouts—most coming in the first three rounds. His only loss was to Marty Marshall years earlier, when Marshall won a narrow decision. Marshall hit Liston hard enough to break his jaw in three places, but never knocked him off his feet. Liston decisioned Marshall two years later to avenge his solitary setback.

Clay entered the fight a 7-1 underdog. He was 19-0, but had been fighting pro for less than four years. He had attracted a large following with his mouth, earning the nickname The Louisville Lip, but few took him seriously as a contender for Liston's crown.

Tex Maule, writing for *Sports Illustrated*, was suitably impressed with the Liston style after observing him train for the Clay fight.

"When he was able to pin one of them (sparring partners) against the ropes, the attack that followed was animal-like in its savagery and it demonstrated another of Liston's assets; his single-mindedness killer instinct.

"It never occurs to Liston that he may lose a fight. His aim is destruction. He cares less for points than he does for doing damage. This intended violence has given him command both physically and psychologically in past fights, and it has caused his opponents—Floyd Patterson, for example—to fight in terror."

Maule added that Patterson "made the mistake of fighting Liston's fight and was demolished."

Clay also recognized the error of Patterson's ways. He had allowed Liston to intimidate him, change his plans and set the terms of battle. Just as Hector could not conceive of the nature of the confrontation that Achilles had proposed three thousand years earlier, so was Patterson unnerved by Liston's approach to the ensuing battle.

But Clay had other plans. The question was, did he have the ability, both mentally and physically, to pull them off.

There were many who thought not. Sure, they recognized his considerable physical abilities—the lightning hands, the graceful footwork, the fantastic physique, the confidence that frequently appeared to slip over into arrogance. But could this young man keep his poise; could he somehow gain the mental edge over the awesome Liston, and then, somehow, hang onto it for fifteen tough, grueling rounds?

One who thought not was Howard Cosell, a still relatively unknown sportscaster in 1964.

"I was one of the many who subscribed to the Liston Mystique," wrote Cosell in his autobiography. "The baleful stare, the huge head wrapped in the towel, all the rest."

Cosell related a frightening encounter with Liston when he was in training for Patterson. Cosell and Rocky Marciano, the retired undefeated heavyweight champ, drove to Aurora Downs, a battered, old and deserted racetrack near Chicago where Liston had set up camp. Talking their way past an armed guard, the two entered the training area where Liston was skipping rope to the record Night Train. Cosell described the scene as "eerie," and said even Marciano was ill at ease. When Cosell suggested that Marciano approach Liston, who was staring at them with a threatening glare, Marciano responded, "I want no part of it. Do you think I'm nuts?"

That's the sort of reputation Liston carried into his fight with the brash Clay. But it only took seven rounds for Clay to destroy the myth of Liston's invincibility and to establish himself as one of the greatest athletes of all time, and the absolute master of arousal techniques.

Clay began a long psychological warfare against Liston, calling him "The Big Ugly Bear" and harrassing him whenever possible. Not only did Clay act unimpressed, he said he was unimpressed. He once drove from Louisville to Denver and stood outside Liston's bedroom window calling him names in the middle of the night. When Liston appeared at the door in night clothes, the police also arrived. Conveniently, Clay had called the police and the media prior to waking Liston, making sure he would get plenty of newspaper coverage . . . and protection, if needed, from the

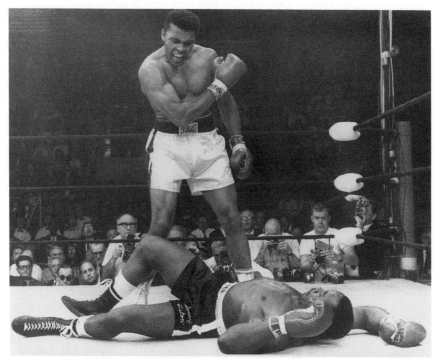

**A young and angry Muhammad Ali yells at a prone Sonny Liston in the second matchup between heavyweight champions May 25, 1965, in Lewiston, Maine. The controversial ending came just sixty seconds into the fight, with Liston going to the canvas for the first time in his career after being hit in the head by a right hand from Ali. (Wide World Photos)**

irate Liston. Clay's manipulations to strip Liston of his overwhelming self-confidence and mental edge was climaxed at the weigh-in scene, which may be the ultimate example of one athlete taking charge of another mentally. Clay yelled and screamed at Liston in such a wild manner that many veteran observers felt he had truly cracked under the pressure of facing Liston. Several suggested that the fight should be cancelled due to Clay's hysterical behavior.

Cosell said the ". . . famous scene at the weigh-in was like something out of the Mad Hatter. Sugar Ray Robinson, restraining him. Drew Brown, one of his handlers, who called himself Bundini, restraining him. All the while, Clay going through this act of apparent insanity, gesturing and screaming at Liston, leaping around the room. The blood pressure was way up. Everyone who saw him wondered if he had truly popped his cork out of fear."

Cosell was unsure at this point whether Clay was acting, or had gone berzerk. But that night, just before the big fignt, he saw Clay catching his younger brother, Rudy, fighting in a preliminary, and was stunned at Clay's

55

poise and cool demeanor. Cosell asked him how there could be such a difference between the weigh-in antics and the "new" Clay.

"He looked at me, winked and said, 'I wanted Liston to know I was crazy,' " wrote Cosell. " 'Only a fool isn't scared of a crazy man. You'll see tonight.' "

Clay boxed Liston silly. He had a perfect fight plan. Weeks before, Clay had written an article for *Sports Illustrated* outlining his strategy.

". . . I am not fooled by what Liston did to Patterson once they started to fight. Liston didn't do anything except hit Floyd while he stood there and took it. Now don't think even for a little bit I'm going to stand around for Liston to do with as he pleases."

Clay's plan was to move—float like a butterfly, sting like a bee, and tire Liston out. Sonny was not used to going the full fifteen rounds, especially at the speed Clay would impose on him. The heavy muscles of Liston would start to fatigue along about the seventh or eighth round, Clay figured, and then the kid from Louisville would go to work. It was a similar strategy that the man known as Muhammad Ali would employ a decade later in Africa against another massively-muscled warrior, and with the same result.

Ali's antics at the weigh-in served two purposes. The first was to make Liston think he was fighting a madman—one who was totally unpredict-able and unafraid. The second was to turn Liston into a seething cauldron of rage. Anger can be an effective force when controlled, as can arousal, but out of control, both wreak havoc. This particular night, Liston's anger was out of control; but Clay's arousal was in perfect control.

"A full commitment to observing yourself and then doing what is necessary to perform better is crucial," said Kauss, adding "The real task involves not avoiding or creating anxiety before competition, but using it in controlled doses. In sport, anxiety has the reputation of being both a crippler of sensitive performers and a motivator of athletes."

Writing about the weigh-in years later, Ali confessed, "The truth of the matter is I've rehearsed and planned every move I make that day . . . Liston has decided he will annihilate me in the first round and I've decided I won't wait for the first round. I'll attack at the weigh-in. I'll act totally crazy and so will Bundini, who is an expert on craziness."

Later, he told his doctor, "Liston has been boasting he's afraid of no man alive. But Liston means no sane man. Liston's got to be afraid of a crazy man."

Anger works on much the same principal as anxiety. If the athlete controls it, anger can prove extremely motivating. If the anger controls the athlete, he is in trouble.

"Even Liston's rage, which took from him most of his boxing ability, had been a part of Clay's strategy," wrote Maule after the fight. "The boasting and calculated gibes with which Clay had irritated Liston during the weeks before the fight had seemed the overweening confidence of a child. Clay had hoodwinked the sportswriters, fans, even members of the combine which owns him. At the weigh-in, he had put on a long, hysterical show, also designed to upset Liston.

"Before the fight, Liston had seemed imperturbable. But in the first round, all the smoldering resentment came out in a rush."

Anger had gotten the best of Sonny Liston. Unless he could catch Clay with an early blow that would turn the fight dramatically in his favor, he was in for a rough evening. Clay moved with precision, flicking his left jab—rated the second best in heavyweight history by Nat Fleischer—into Liston's face time and again, scoring points, inflicting punishment and causing untold mental depression.

Liston's face began to swell, and he began to bleed and to move away from Clay. "His expression was puzzled and shocked and almost frightened," wrote Maule. "The arrogant self-confidence that, in previous fights, had allowed him to dominate his opponents, was gone."

Then Clay applied the final strokes in his demolishing of Liston's ego. He began to yell at him, to taunt him: "Come on and fight, you bum!" He was now in complete control.

"Clay was boxing Liston all over the ring . . . suddenly I was in the process of seeing the Big Black Bear exposed," wrote Cosell. "Now out of nowhere the left side of Liston's face was slit from the eye down to the lip. It was like a zipper and out gushed the blood, which he tasted. Rocky Marciano, who was doing the fight with me, leaned over and said, 'He's become an old man.' "

It was the culmination of months of planning by Clay. He had crafted a plan, much like Gene Tunney had when he went after Jack Dempsey nearly forty years earlier, and executed it to perfection. The plan was nursed along carefully by Clay and put into fruition in the ring. He worked on the fragile elements of Liston's self perception, letting him know that he, Clay, was not going to fall prey to the Liston mystique and buildup. If you are going to beat me, Clay told him by his actions, you're going to have to do it with your fists, not with your reputation.

Then, Clay used Liston's rage against him, making sure the Bear would forget any fight plan devised and go after him with murder in his heart. Clay knew he had the physical equipment—height, speed and hand quickness—to keep Liston at bay. Others had done it, and Clay knew he could too. As he had noted earlier, Patterson had fought him all wrong; Clay would never repeat that mistake.

The second Ali-Liston fight is an enigma. Cosell wrote that Liston looked even better physically for that fight than the first one. Yet the fight ended within sixty seconds in the first round under a cloud of suspicion. Liston, a man who had never been off his feet, was knocked out by a punch hardly anyone saw.

Referee Jersey Joe Walcott was adamant about the punch: "The right hand punch that Clay dropped Liston with is one of the most devastating punches I've ever seen; Sonny was hurt real bad."

The fights with Clay tarnished the Liston image badly, and probably for all time. But Ali, as the years passed, gave full credit to Liston, saying he was a great fighter.

In the book *Superfists*, Graham Houston paid Liston the tribute he deserves: "Most people will probably remember Sonny Liston as the heavyweight champion who was twice humiliated by brash Cassius Clay. Despite this Liston emerges as one of the most formidable heavyweights in history . . . at his best, (he) could have been expected to give any champion in history a very uncomfortable evening."

Ali encountered a foe very similar to Liston in his last great fight. George Foreman possessed a 40-0 record and the highest knockout percentage in heavyweight history (37 kayos in his 40 fights) when he defended his title against Ali October 30, 1974. Ali called it "the rumble in the jungle," and he played with Foreman's mind in a manner reminiscent of the Liston clashes. He taunted him constantly, calling him a paper tiger with no punch.

Earlier, Foreman had admitted that he considered himself a young Liston, and would avenge Sonny's loss to Ali. "He loved Liston," wrote Ali in his autobiography. "He was impressed by Liston's brute force and power. And he has captured most of it and more . . ."

As the two fighters received their instructions in the ring, Ali was reminded again of Liston: "Our eyes were locked like gunfighters in a Wild West movie. Angelo (Dundee) and Bundini (Drew Brown) rub my shoulders. Sandy (Saddler) and Archie (Moore) stand with George. In his eyes, I see Sonny Liston glaring at me ten years ago at Miami Beach, a fresh, young, powerful, taller, stronger Liston."

Ali went to work immediately. He leaned close to Foreman and called him a chump, saying he was going to be embarrassed. He used the same psychology on Foreman that worked so well on Liston: the object was to drive George into a slow rage, one that would convert him from a methodical boxer into a nonthinking brawler dead set upon annihilation. "Come on sucker, show me something, chump . . . they say you hit hard . . . is that the best you can do sissy?"

But the game plan almost backfired. This was not the Ali of the flashing hands and feet of ten years ago, but one considerably slower and flat of foot. This time he fought more with heart and desire, mixed with hard experience, than with raw, savage skills. But he still had the mental edge and would not surrender it that particular night, even though Foreman hurt him desperately in the second round.

Ali, exhibiting the ring genius that made him such a remarkable champion, changed his strategy and instead of running from Foreman, dropped to the ropes and absorbed his punches. It was the rope-a-dope, and Ali used it to perfection, exhibiting incredible courage. Who in their right mind would stand stationary and invite George Foreman, the man who annihilated Joe Frazier, to punch away? Only Ali . . .

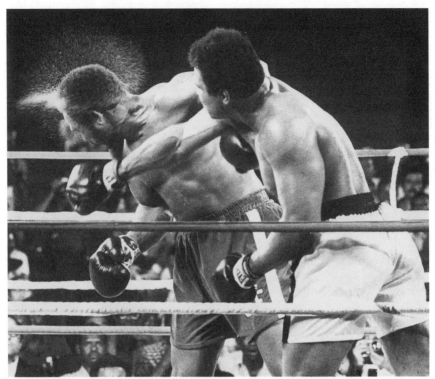

**Muhammad Ali lands a crunching right hand to the head of champion George Foreman during their October 30, 1974, title fight in Kinshasa, Zaire. Ali stunned the boxing world by handing Foreman his first loss in 41 bouts with an eighth-round knockout. (Wide World Photos)**

"I feel his breath coming in gasps and I know I'm taking something out of him," said Ali. "I know this round will go down on the judges' scorecards as belonging to George, but there's something in it that belongs to me."

And Ali continued to work on Foreman's mind. Near the end of the seventh round, a round Foreman hadn't been extended to in his previous twelve bouts, Ali reminded him that he has eight more to go. "I ain't even got started, and you out of breath," snarled the ex-champ. "Look at you! Out of gas, and I'm whipping you."

The psychological ramifications of such words, if they have a ring of truth, can be crushing. Ali knew Foreman wanted to remain champ, but he was wondering if he would pay the price. Could he suck it up like Ali had to on numerous occasions?

In the eighth round, Ali slammed a terrific right to Foreman's chin. It was Ali's first great blow of the fight, and Foreman toppled like a big oak tree. But the punch only finished what Ali had started much earlier. The annihilation of Foreman's mental side was begun weeks before the fight, and carried through expertly during the first seven rounds. Exhausted,

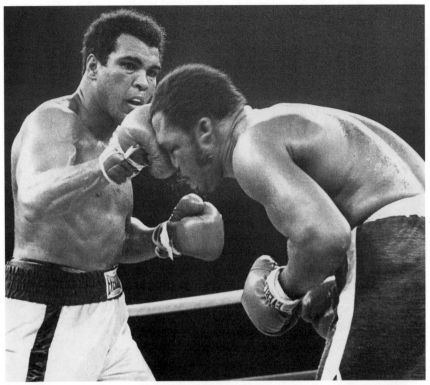

**Joe Frazier, one-time world heavyweight boxing champion, takes a stiff right to the head from Muhammad Ali during their 1975 title fight in Manila. Ali retained his title when Frazier failed to answer the bell for the fifteenth round. It was the third meeting between the two valiant warriors, and gave Ali a 2-1 edge in the series, which was regarded as one of the best in ring history. (Wide World Photos)**

both physically and mentally, Foreman was finished when the first telling blow landed. This victory, like the first one over Liston, was as much mental as physical.

Liston and Foreman are the proof of Ali's true genius. Two of the most formidable heavyweights of all time—ferocious punchers who sent chills down the spines of ordinary fighters—they were easy pickings for the combined mental and physical skills of Ali.

But Joe Frazier was another matter. The Ali genius didn't work on this man who exhibited a raw courage equal to that of Dempsey, Tunney and Marciano. His heart was too big to allow Ali to weaken it with his quips, suggestions and digs. His personality, bolstered by a true confidence, was too well fortified to allow Ali to slice into it.

A fascinating angle to the great Frazier-Ali fights is the auto trip the two took together before their first bout. Frazier was driving to New York on business, and Ali, still in forced exile for his refusal to be inducted into the armed services, hitched a ride with him. For the entire trip, each man tried to gain the mental edge over the other, knowing its value if they should ever battle. Neither, however, was able to gain an advantage.

At one point Ali, testing Frazier's mettle, said "If we can't get along, let's get it on."

"We'll get it on," replied Frazier coolly. "Ain't no doubt about that. Because once the bell rings . . . See, you get out there and try to psych them guys. Me, I'm different. I'm the greatest psych artist ever put on this earth. You outpsych Houdini easier than me . . ."

The first titanic fight between these two champions came March 8, 1971. Ali's layoff was too much, and Frazier fought a brilliant battle, taking a 15-round decision. But Ali won the rematch, a 12-rounder, January 28, 1974. And the rubber bout, fought October 1, 1975, in Manilla also went to Ali. He hurt Frazier desperately in the second, and showed incredible courage and heart as he outlasted Frazier, who was unable to answer the bell for the final round. Ali said it was the closest he ever came to dying.

Frazier was the fighter Ali respected the most. "Frazier was the most ruthless, agressive and competitive heavyweight in modern times," wrote Ali. Once, watching Foreman struggling to stand in the eighth round, Ali's thoughts reverted to Frazier: "I watch every lift of the referee's arm. I remember thinking again of Frazier. He would never lose the crown lying on the floor. No referee could count over his body as long as he had blood in it."

He's right. And no man could psych out Frazier, either. In that respect, he was a whole level above Liston and Foreman.

But Ali was on a different plateau than any other heavyweight boxer ever. His physical tools were unmatched in boxing history. From Bruce Lee to Dan Gable, he was respected by all the great champions in other fields. Walcott, who saw the legendary Dempsey, Louis and Marciano— and fought the last two — said Ali, in his prime, was the best ever.

Before his exile, Ali was as close to being unbeatable as any heavyweight ever was. After the layoff, he was still good enough to defeat Frazier twice and Foreman once, and to take two out of three from Ken Norton, a tough heavyweight in anyone's book.

"Ali was the master of the psych," said Angelo Dundee, his trainer and one of boxing's most recognized experts. "There was that famous scene before the weigh-in of the first Liston fight. Muhammad was screaming and carrying on he wanted to get at 'The Big Ugly Bear' right now. Well, it was all staged. I was holding Muhammad off with my pinkie."

Ali will be remembered, as the years slip by, as one of the greatest fighters to ever lace on a glove. And one of the smartest. He was a man who could outthink his foe, outbox him, or outslug him. He was, as he was prone to say himself, "The Greatest."

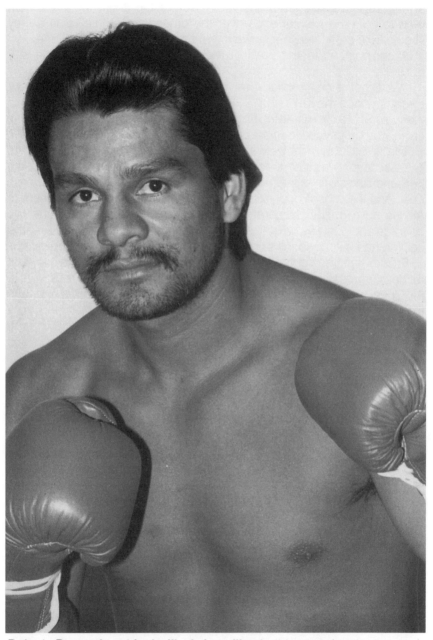

Roberto Duran almost looks like he's smiling in this staged photo, but very few of his opponents ever saw the Panamanian terror smile in the ring. Duran was world lightweight champion for seven years, and then won the world welterweight title in 1980 with a hard-fought decision over Sugar Ray Leonard. Duran was regarded one of the best—and meanest—fighters of all time and was 72-1 after his win over Leonard.

# ROBERTO DURAN

# The Angry Panamanian

"Is this man too nice to fight?" asked the editors of *Inside Sports* on the cover of the March, 1982 magazine. Displayed with the words was a large photo of a semi-smiling Gerry Cooney, the one-time leading contender for the world heavyweight boxing title.

Being "too nice" can be a handicap in a number of sports, and particularly boxing, a discipline which demands a certain amount of hostility. A boxer must have "killer instinct" in the ring, regardless of his natural personality traits outside the ring. Ray Leonard is a perfect example of a figher who has the ability to be engaging and affable outside the roped arena, and cold and calculated inside the ring. To be a successful prizefighter means to be mean and nasty, at least part of the time.

"True talent won't win it. The folks that put it together between their ears, get tough and mean and ornery—and stay that way—will win it."

The speaker of those words was not a general leading his men into battle. He was Norm Ellenberger, who was, at the time, head basketball coach at the University of New Mexico. He was talking about the race for the league title in the Western Athletic Conference. Ellenberger is gone from the scene, but his words linger on. They fit to perfection many athletes who have been able to excel not because they had great talent, but because they were tough, mean and ornery. The words have never fit a man better than Roberto Duran.

Tough, mean, ornery: they are words that Duran wears well. But there are others. Terrifying, vicious, sadistic. They have all been used at one time to characterize the man that *KO* magazine regards as one of the ten meanest men ever to fight professionally. And that takes in a hell of a lot of territory. It places Duran alongside such men as Jack Dempsey, Harry Greb and Fritzie Zivic, who prided himself on being the dirtiest fighter of all time.

Whether Duran was the meanest man to ever fight is open to debate. But this much is not open—he was at least one of the meanest to ever crawl between the ropes. He epitomized what Ellenberger was talking about, and carried the concept to its farthest extremity. Duran has been called a lot of things in his life, but "too nice" is not among them.

After demolishing world-ranked contender Ray Lampkin with a brutal knockout in 1975, Duran exhibited little concern for the fallen fighter. "If I had been in shape, they'd be taking him to the morgue, not the hospital," he snarled.

"After Duran stopped Pedro Menoza in 1975, a sobbing woman leaped into the ring and began cursing him," said the article on Duran in *KO* magazine. "The fiery brawler reportedly responded by decking her with a right hand."

"He has often been surly with the press and treated their questions with impatience, if not disdain," wrote Tom Archdeacon of the Cox News Service in 1983. "But that is really nothing compared to what Duran has done to his opponents. He treated most of them with contempt before the fight, and once he got them in the ring he usually battered them with an animalistic savagery."

No, Duran is not—at least while immersed in the practice of his chosen profession—to be termed a "nice fellow."

But that's as he prefers it. No sport relies more on intimidation than boxing, and perhaps no sport relies more on the mental warfare that rages inside of two combatants. It's a brutal endeavor; for most purposes, the object is not to outpoint the other man, for you may do that for nine rounds and then get knocked stiff in the tenth, and lose. It's happened a thousand times; therefore, the object is to render the foe unconscious as soon as possible.

Ira Berkow, writing for *The New York Times* Service, related a tale of how effective mental warfare can be in a prizefighter. "The last time this reporter saw (Archie) Moore was in June of 1973 when Moore was in the corner of Ernie Shavers, who knocked out Jimmy Ellis in the first round in Madison Square Garden.

"Moore, a believer in psychological ploys, recalled the advice he had given Shavers. At the weigh-in, the two fighters met and Ellis, conventionally, extended his hand to shake. But Shavers grabbed Ellis' forearm and said, 'You're in trouble, boy.' "

" 'Ellis,' said Moore, laughing, 'never recovered.' "

Duran grabbed his foes' minds, and never allowed them to recover. He grew up in the worst slums of Panama, sleeping in the streets at night, fighting in them by day. He was a notorious street fighter, and developed a reputation for his willingness to take on anyone, any time.

In many respects he was a much smaller, modern-day version of Jack Dempsey, who fought and brawled his way through the mining towns of the Rocky Mountain west, hungry to earn a meal and a reputation, eager to find a spot in a society that turned its back on him. Duran was molded from the same background that made America's greatest early fighers ornery and vicious.

Duran had his first professional fight March 8, 1967, earning a four-round decision over Carlos Mendoza in Colon, Panama. He flattened each of his next four opponents in the first round, and had a total of eight consecutive knockouts before earning another decision on September 4, 1968. In his twentyeighth professional fight, he became the world's lightweight champion by stopping the game and gutty Ken Buchanan of Scotland in the thirteenth round in New York City. The date was June 26, 1972; Duran had been a professional fighter for over five years.

Controversy surrounded the Buchanan fight, as the Scotsman claimed that Duran had repeatedly hit him low. But Duran's nonstop body attack was the key to the victory, and Buchanan had been solidly behind on all the officials' cards.

Duran returned to Panama as the champion of the world, and scored first round knockouts in his next two matches, bringing his record to 30-0. But then he suffered his first defeat, losing a ten-round decision to Estaban DeJesus. The slick Puerto Rican decked Duran in the first round and held on to take the decision. It was a loss that Duran would later avenge twice. The second fight with DeJesus came March 16, 1974, and again Duran hit the canvas early. But he roared back to score a knockout in the eleventh. Nearly four years later, he stopped DeJesus in the twelfth round.

After defending his title twelve times and scoring a record-setting nine consecutive kayoes in lightweight title defenses, Duran elected to move on to bigger tasks. In 1979 he pounded out a clear decision over Carlos Palomino, the skilled former welterweight champion of the world, and set his sights on Sugar Ray Leonard, the darling of the 1976 Olympics and undefeated world welterweight champion.

June 20, 1980, marked the apex of the Duran career. Waging an almost perfect fight against one of the finest craftsmen in ring history, the man from Panama became a world champion for the second time. Battling the Sugar Man tooth and nail for fifteen rounds, Duran earned a tough, but clear, decision. His record was now 72-1, with 55 knockouts. In the opinion of most experts, he was one of the two greatest lightweights of all time, sharing that honor with the legendary Benny Leonard.

In a February, 1983 issue of *KO* magazine, he ranked fifth among the greatest boxers, regardless of weight division, since 1940. The only men ranked ahead of him were (in order) Ray Robinson, Muhammad Ali, Willie Pep and Joe Louis. Listed behind him were such magnificent fighters as Carlos Monzon, Henry Armstrong, Ray Leonard, Jose Napoles, Rocky Marciano, Archie Moore, Alexis Arguello and Larry Holmes.

*KO* magazine called Duran "a fighting machine from the slums of Panama who grew into as fierce and determined a champion as boxing has ever seen . . . combined fine boxing skills and excellent hand speed with a fearless, aggressive attack to intimidate and overwhelm most foes."

Duran, as a fighter, was a personification of all the qualities that make a boxer great. He exhibited the total fearlessness of Marciano, the hunger and savagery of Dempsey, the arousal techniques of Muhammad Ali, and the ability to control his feelings that enabled Tunney to excel. At the time of his conquest over Leonard, Duran might have been as close to unbeatable as a fighter could be.

But the single quality that seemed to most characterize Duran was the intensity with which he fought—an intensity that was apparently born of anger. When the Panamanian entered the ring he appeared angry and acted angry. He snarled, growled, glared and stomped. After the final bell rang at the first Leonard fight, he actually spat in the face of Leonard, who was offering congratulations. Even in his finest moment, Duran could not contain the anger that had enabled him to fight with such ferocity.

"It is a fact . . . that many athletes, especially professionals and those involved in physically punishing sports that are derived from fighting (wrestling, boxing, and to some extent football), use hate and anger as a source of arousal, often with much success," wrote David R. Kauss in his book, *Peak Performance.*

"In using anger as a source of arousal, we can provide a real or imagined object of frustration, allow anger to build, and then release the arousal along with the anger in competition, against an object (the opponent) we can do something about."

One athlete who discovered the power of using controlled doses of anger—long before Duran was even born—was Bill Koll, a three-time national wrestling champion at Iowa State Teachers College in 1946, 1947 and 1948. Koll finished his collegiate career with a 72-0 record, and was twice named the outstanding wrestler at the national meet. Today, nearly four decades after his last match, wrestling fans still discuss his ability to psych himself up for each match he entered.

"It was during the freshman season that I also realized that directing and controlling one's arousal to competition could be as important as learning skills," said Koll recently. "I discovered that if I could focus my anger towards some incident, some object, event or person that my state of readiness and overall performance was increased. My strength, speed and ability to think were increased tremendously by just sitting apart from the action prior to the match and getting into a state of controlled anger. The key is that I was always in control of the anger and never allowed it to control me."

Duran epitomized anger in action. And the anger found expression in his eyes, as well as his hammering fists.

"He's got them eyes—like an animal, like he wants to kill you," said Freddie Brown, a trainer with a legendary reputation. "No matter who fights Duran, they gotta fear him."

After Duran beat Leonard, former heavyweight champion Joe Frazier, a tough man himself, said that Duran reminded him of Charles Manson, one of this century's most feared criminals, and a man who spooked even hardened journalists with his maniacal stare.

In the summer of 1980, Duran was riding a crest of fame unmatched among recent smaller fighters. His record was almost perfect. The aura surrounding him was one few men have ever enjoyed. And then came November 25, 1980, and the rematch with Sugar Ray Leonard. For as long as men discuss pugilism, this fight will be remembered. In terms of controversial endings, it ranks second only to the Gene Tunney-Jack Dempsey fight of "long count" fame.

Duran, the man who would never quit, the man who would never give up, the man they called "Hands of Stone" and a man considered far and wide to be one of the most competitive athletes who ever lived, quit. Near the end of the eighth round, Duran smiled quickly and threw up his gloved hands, telling referee Octavio Meyran and a stunned world that he was through for the evening.

The words "No mas" (meaning no more) echoed around the world. The unthinkable had happened. Roberto Duran had not only lost a fight— the first one in nearly eight years—but he had *quit*.

Countless articles have been written about the fight. Every fight magazine in the world offered its explanations and analysis. His trainer, Ray Arcel—one of the truly legendary figures of boxing, a man who had been around the sport for over sixty years and who is respected by absolutely everyone in the game—walked away, shaking his head. He said that he could never offer an explanation, and that he was quitting the sport. He had seen it all when he had seen Roberto Duran quit.

The fight was close at the time, though Leonard was leading on all cards. There was plenty of time for a comeback, and Duran was known as a fighter who came on strong in the late rounds.

Only Duran had an explanation. He said he was suffering from stomach cramps.

"The day of the fight I did not feel physically fit," Duran told *Ring* magazine writer Randy Gordon. "In the ring I had pains—terrible pains—in my stomach. I did what I did because I could not continue fighting. I was ill, I was sick. I couldn't do anything else. I would never give up against anybody."

No, Duran would not give up against anybody. But he might give up against something. For years, he had fought with a ravaging hunger, a need to prove himself, to be somebody. That need had driven him, like a man obsessed, pushing him to the very top. He was wealthy beyond his wildest dreams. But Duran never fought for money; he fought for glory, and to satisfy the hunger that dwelled deep within his soul.

"Games are a sublimation of combat between individuals or between cities, regions or countries," wrote Thomas Tutko, Ph.D., in his book, *Sports Psyching*. "As great warriors have always been great heroes, the warriors of our time, the professional athletes, now often receive the social benefits of generals."

That was true of Duran in Panama. He was a national hero of the very highest standing. Only such an overwhelming success could calm the anger and frustration that burned inside him. A subdued Duran, one without the fury of his younger days, could, perhaps, be beaten—inwardly, if not outwardly. Just as Rome crumbled from within, so do many great fighters.

"I knew I'd have trouble getting into top shape and cutting the weight so fast," said Duran, who had ballooned up to 180 pounds after his victory over Leonard. As a lightweight just two years earlier, he had been forced to make the 135-pound limit. Against Leonard, he had weighed-in at 147 pounds.

Then, Duran spoke from the heart: "My mental attitude was not as it should have been."

Of that, there can be little doubt. His anger, the key element of his success, had at last subsided, and with it went another huge ally—confidence.

"Confidence is a key word in describing Duran in and out of the ring," explained Jim Duschen, a former national wrestling champion who has ushered at a number of the biggest fights in Las Vegas for nearly eight years. "Once in the ring, he's there for one purpose, and that's to take his opponent apart. He is very intense, almost angry, due to his highly-competitive nature. At close range, you can tell by the look on his face how determined he is. He appears to be staring right through his opponent.

"Roberto has a great savvy and natural instinct as to when to attack. He is definitely as mentally tough as anyone I've ever seen in sports."

After the second fight, Duran and Leonard went different ways. Leonard defended against Thomas Hearns in one of the most gruelling fights of the decade, giving the Hitman his first loss and winning by a technical knockout in the fourteenth round. He retired shortly thereafter due to complications from an eye injury. One of boxing's finest men in and out of the ring, Leonard could look back on a professional record of 32-1 and remember stirring victories over such terrific battlers as Duran, Hearns, and Wilfred Benitez. His single loss was to Duran.

But the "Hands of Stone" from Panama landed on tough times. In the two years following the Leonard fight, he climbed into the ring seven times and won just five of those bouts. Something had indeed happened to the legendary Duran.

Some experts said he was too big, too slow and on the downward side of a great career. Even a stirring fourth-round knockout of the once-

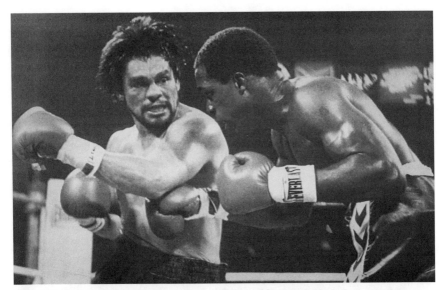

**Roberto Duran (left) pounds away at Davey Moore during their world junior middleweight championship bout at Madison Square Garden in June of 1983. Duran stopped Moore in the eighth round to win his third world championship. (Associated Press Photo)**

feared Pipino Cuevas, former world champion, on January 29, 1983 brought few hurrahs.

"I'm coming back to show the world there is no way Leonard can beat me," said Duran nearly a year after the second fight with Leonard. "On his best night he couldn't beat me. He didn't beat me in our first fight. How can he beat me unless I'm sick . . ."

Redemption came at last in the person of Davey Moore, the young and undefeated junior middleweight champion of the world. Duran, showing an intensity that many had thought was lost forever, turned in another savage performance, battering Moore at will and scoring a dramatic eight-round knockout. On June 16, 1983 a frenzied, full-house audience at Madison Square Garden saw the Duran of old. With the victory he became just the sixth man in boxing history to win three different world titles in a career.

Unless Leonard is willing to risk permanent injury to his eyes and return to the ring, Leonard and Duran will never slug it out again. Now Duran has to be content with the glory he reclaimed against Moore. He need not fret overly long on his one inglorious moment in the ring; there were far too many victories and knockouts to let one loss sour the years of triumph.

Boxing fans will always remember the image of a snarling, stalking fighter, bound up with a passion and an energy that was undeniable, and intent upon releasing an anger that might have consumed him had he not released it in the ring.

**A 1910 studio portrait of the magnificent Frank Gotch, considered by most experts to be the greatest professional wrestler of all time. Gotch was world champion from 1908 until his retirement in 1915 and was a friend of boxing champions James J. Jeffries and Gentleman Jim Corbett. Gotch stood just under six feet tall and weighed 212 pounds at his peak.**

# FRANK GOTCH

# A Champion Of Confidence

The later 1880s were a wild and wooly period, and the state of Iowa sat precariously on the edge of the frontier, bordering between the "civilized" east and the "uncivilized" west. It was a period and place that bred strong and hardy men.

The Indian wars were just playing themselves out, and the short-lived era of the gunfighter was about to expire. There were few organized sports. Baseball and football were in their infancy, and basketball had not yet been conceived.

The sports idols of most Americans were bare-knuckle prizefighters and catch-as-catch-can grapplers. Both types of rugged athletes barnstormed through the Midwest, looking for "pickup" bouts where small wagers could be made. Rugged and seasoned athletes made their rounds, taking on the local sports heroes in often brutal engagements.

The game was tough, full of hard knocks and busted noggins. Those who survived became heroes; those who excelled became legends.

Frank Gotch was one who excelled.

Born in 1878 on a farm near Humboldt, a small town in northwest Iowa, Gotch was adept at all the sports of his day. He loved track and enjoyed baseball. But his specialty was wrestling. He became, in a short amount of time, and in the opinion of nearly all experts, the greatest professional wrestler the world has ever seen.

Even the legendary Ed "Stranger" Lewis, who earned his fearsome nickname because of his habit of nearly strangling men with his vicious side headlock, didn't mince words when he discussed his spot in the hierarchy of all-time great wrestlers.

"I wasn't a Frank Gotch, but then nobody else was either," said the crusty Lewis, who was, for years, the world's champion in the 1930s and

**Frank Gotch works a double arm lever on a foe during a studio practice session in 1910. Gotch, an Iowa farmboy, became the nation's No. 1 sports hero during his reign as world heavyweight wrestling champion from 1908 to 1915.**

'40s. "I tried to come closest, and maybe I did. I hope so."

Lewis did come as close as anyone to matching Gotch, but he was a long way off. Gotch was in a class by himself.

Gotch first earned his reputation as a wrestler by beating an older man known locally as the "Chicken Picker." It gained Gotch—then just nineteen—a local reputation, and he was the natural choice to wrestle a cocky stranger who came to the area one hot summer day in 1899. The stranger issued a challenge to wrestle to a group of boys and young men running track, and Gotch stepped forward.

The stranger was Dan McLeod, the reigning American champion. It was a "pickup" bout, and the Iowans were completely unaware of who it was they were sending their man out to face. When McLeod suggested they wrestle in the grass, Gotch surprised him by demanding that they wrestle on the cinder track instead. For one hour and twenty minutes they went at it, tooth and nail, rolling in the cinders, perspiring heavily, bleeding and puffing. Eventually McLeod's skills won out, and he pinned Gotch's shoulders to the track, gaining the fall and the victory.

It was an excruciatingly painful loss for Gotch, but it whetted his appetite for more wrestling. Shortly after, he met the famed Farmer Burns, perhaps the most knowledgeable wrestler to ever walk the earth. Many years older than Gotch, Burns was about ready to step down from big-time wrestling and took Gotch under his wing. The two were to prove an unbeatable combination.

Armed with his own immense strength and a quickness that was stunning for a big man, Gotch studied all aspects of wrestling under Burns. When the time was ripe, he left Iowa and headed north, settling in Dawson, Alaska. There, living and working with the rugged men of the mining camps, Gotch cleaned up the Yukon. With little else for entertainment, the miners took to sporting events—primarily boxing and wrestling. Gotch won every match he fought, and returned to Iowa six months later with nearly $35,000 in winnings—most of it earned through bets he placed on himself.

Back in the states, Gotch longed for the American championship, and went after it. The title was held by Tom Jenkins, one of the roughest wrestlers of all time. The one-eyed Cleveland millwright had been champ for a number of years, and had no intention of relinquishing the title to Gotch. In one of the roughest wrestling matches of all time, Jenkins emerged victorious after an hour of pitched battle.

"Gotch was a sorry sight as he returned to his home," reads his 1913 biography, "bruised and bandaged, his nose twisted and his body decorated with plasters and other reminders of the battle. Referee Edwards at one point threatened to stop the match. He told the wrestlers he was there to referee a mat battle, not a prize fight or a cock fight."

In those days, professional wrestling was a far cry from the professional wrestling of today. It was very similar to amateur wrestling, with two

**Frank Gotch (left), American wrestling champion, shakes hands with the legendary Russian Lion, George Hackenschmidt, prior to the start of their epic match in Chicago in 1911. The referee is Edward Smith, a Chicago sportswriter.**

exceptions: there was seldom a time limit, and the accent was on the submission hold rather than the pin. There was also a lot of mat wrestling, which, in itself, can be boring, and which eventually led to the decline of true professional wrestling and the introduction of theatrics. But in the days of Gotch and Jenkins, a wrestling match was similar to a legalized street fight, with few restrictions.

Gotch trained for his rematch with Jenkins with a vengeance. He played handball to sharpen his reflexes, worked with pulleys, and ran long distances—some days up to thirty miles, broken down to distances of five to ten miles at a crack. He was one of the very first athletes to put a premium on conditioning, and to incorporate long runs into his training sessions. The work paid off.

**In a rare photograph, Frank Gotch (left) and George Hackenschmidt tie up during their world championship wrestling match in Chicago in 1911. The two men are ranked one-two, respectively, by Nat Fleisher on the list of all-time greatest wrestlers. This match drew a crowd of approximately 30,000 fans.**

"This match wasn't a scientific grappling contest," wrote Gotch's manager, Emil Klank, years later. "It was a rough and tumble encounter. If I live to be a hundred years old, I never expect to see a mat struggle the likes of that one between Gotch and Jenkins."

With Gotch's victory, wrestling in America entered a new era. Gotch, who was handsome and articulate, became the number one sports hero in America. His picture was on the cover of the leading sports journals of the day; farm implements and a cigar were named after him; and his name became synonymous with strength. But Gotch went after still larger laurels. With America conquered, he turned his gaze toward Europe, home of the famed Russian Lion.

George Hackenschmidt came out of Estonia and Russia to earn honors that are staggering when comtemplated eight decades later. At one point, he was the weightlifting champion of Russia, and he set world records in the lifting of heavy objects. His physique was marvelous, with muscles bulging and rippling. In addition, he had a keen mind, being fluent in seven languages. Later in life, he wrote a number of books, including such titles as *Man and Cosmic Antagonism to Mind and Spirit*, *Consciousness and Character*, and *The Three Memories of Forgetfulness*. He even debated the esteemed George Bernard Shaw to a standstill, and challenged Albert Einstein to discuss his theory of relativity.

Hackenschmidt gained his greatest fame, however, as one of the two greatest wrestlers of all time. He set Europe on its athletic ear at the turn of the century with his impressive wrestling victories. He was so powerful that even the greatest European wrestlers were helpless in his hands. He drew huge crowds wherever he appeared, but especially in London. He frequently wrestled three or four wrestlers in a single night, dispatching them with ease.

Perhaps his most famous European match came against Madrali, known as "The Terrible Turk." A huge man, Madrali had blown away competition about as easily as Hackenschmidt. When they met at the Olympia Opera House in London, it was an overflow crowd of top society—the men in tails and top hats, the women in elegant gowns. Everyone was eager to see who was the continent's greatest wrestler. Hackenschmidt, who would "carry" no one, decked the terrible Turk in two minutes flat. He then proceeded to easily defeat the American champ, Jenkins, twice.

When Hackenschmidt came to America to meet Gotch in 1908, hardly anyone gave the American grappler a chance. But Gotch returned to the training methods he had used for Jenkins, and worked himself into a physical condition that would only be matched by amateur wrestler Dan Gable and professional boxer Rocky Marciano in recent years.

Gotch's strategy was to overhook the Russian's head, to lean on him, and to tire him out. The plan worked, and after over two hours of wrestling, Hackenschmidt gave up the match, and the title. Suddenly, an Iowa farm boy was the heavyweight wrestling champion of the world.

Gotch, already wealthy, starred in a play that toured the east coast and Europe. He invested his money in rich Iowa farmland, and in Minnesota land. He branched off into a number of businesses and became even wealthier, but he continued to wrestle, destroying foe after foe, often with ridiculous ease. He became close friends with former world boxing champion James J. Jeffries, and even contemplated taking up a pro boxing career. At one point, Jeffries himself pushed for a match between the two.

"Jeff has picked out the three challengers most deserving of attention, and suggested the challenger for his title come from them," said a news article of the day. 'Let these three men fight it out and I will take the best,' " said Jeffries. The three men were former heavyweight champion Bob Fitzsimmons, heavyweight champion-to-be Marvin Hart, and Gotch.

Tom Sharkey, one of the leading contenders for the boxing championship for years, said, "Gotch is the fastest man for his size on his feet I ever saw. He is as nimble as Jim Corbett. In bull strength, I doubt Jeffries surpasses Gotch on any point. Gameness is an essential quality in a fight and there is no doubt that Gotch is game after the many gruelling matches he has gone through successfully on the mat. There are many wrestling matches far more brutal than boxing matches."

A St. Louis writer, assessing Gotch's boxing potential, said, "Any person who has seen Gotch will readily admit that he is the most magnificent athlete in this country. For his weight and massive build he is the fastest man that ever contested for honors in an athletic way."

Gotch actually fought several boxing matches, winning all but one. But he returned to wrestling to meet a challenge from Hackenschmidt, who claimed Gotch had used foul methods in their first match. The second bout was held in Chicago's Comiskey Park, in 1913, with nearly 30,000 fans looking on. The event warranted front page coverage on nearly every major newspaper in America, and telegraph stations were set up to relay the score. The result was another victory by Gotch, this time easier than before. He scored two falls over the Russian Lion, and was from then on considered unbeatable. He was invited to the White House by Teddy Roosevelt, and once stripped down to his waist to take on, at the president's request, a ju jitsu expert. Gotch won the impromptu bout easily.

There were several "secrets" to Gotch's success. First, there were his physical attributes.

"Gotch, standing 5 feet 11 and one half inches tall and weighing 212 pounds in his prime, was a remarkable physical specimen," wrote George A. Barton, sports editor of the *Minneapolis Tribune*. "He was tremendously strong, amazingly fast and catlike in movement. Frank was the master of all holds on offense and blocks for these holds on defense. He also mastered leverage to the nth degree and was the last word in courage."

"He was as fast and quick as a lightweight," wrote Sec Taylor, sports editor of the *Des Moines Register*. "His speed was often the dominating factor in his toughest matches, and he had determination and utter disdain of opponents, fear and pain."

While there is no doubt that his physical abilities aided Gotch immensely—particularly his quickness, which was very unusual for a man his size—his most precious asset was his mental outlook. Gotch, as both Barton and Taylor noted, was one of the most fearless athletes ever, and that lack of fear came from a total confidence in himself. Gotch's confident demeanor actually unnerved many of his foes before the bouts even started.

Though Gotch was by all accounts an out-going, affable, friendly sort of guy, he had a confidence that was total and consuming. He was ready to take on anyone, anywhere, anytime—confident of victory.

When he entered the ring for his royal battles with both Jenkins and Hackenschmidt, he smiled broadly, waved to the crowds and "joshed" with his adversaries. It was a trademark he carried throughout his career, which consisted of roughly 400 official matches (with only six losses, all early in his career) and nearly 2,000 pickup bouts, none of which he lost.

A cartoon in a popular Chicago publication of the day showed a smiling Gotch advancing on a fear-struck opponent, arms outstretched and ready to tangle. "He always gets their nanny with that confident smile that won't come off," said the inscription.

World heavyweight wrestling champion Frank Gotch applies his feared toehold on the cover of the April 19, 1913 issue of *The National Police Gazette*. For years, *The National Police Gazette* was the leading sports journal in America, and it often carried large stories and photographs of Gotch.

Almost every newspaper account of the day began with the statement, "Gotch came out with a confident smile."

Just prior to Gotch's first bout with Hackenschmidt, with the world title at stake and the largest crowd in wrestling history on hand, Gotch was as calm as could be: "When we walked into Gotch's room he gave us a merry reception," wrote C.J. Murray, who came in to cover the match from Buffalo, New York. "He was as chipper as a boy starting on a midsummer vacation. He was laughing and chatting with his Iowa friends. Hackenschmidt wasn't worrying him."

When the two wrestling legends began their showdown, Gotch talked to Hackenschmidt continually, teasing him and taunting him. Nearly an hour into the match, with neither man able to gain much of an advantage, Hackenschmidt suggested they settle for a draw. He was accustomed to early, fast pins, and he was losing heart at his inability to master Gotch. Gotch merely laughed, and said they should wrestle for several more hours. The response disheartened the fabled Russian Lion, who realized that Gotch was as fresh as when they started.

After the match, Gotch summed up his victory eloquently:

"I got my first feeling of ultimate victory when we stood up to be photographed before the match began," said Gotch. "I reached out my hand to shake with Hack, and when he took my hand I felt his hand shaking and trembling. And something said to me right then, 'Frank, this fellow is worried,' and it gave me new courage."

Gotch's mental edge went a long way in his victory, but so did his ability to understand the technique of negating a strong man's power. There is little doubt that Hackenschmidt was the strongest professional wrestler of all time, yet Gotch effectively took away that advantage.

"I made Hack reach for me all the time, and never did he get a chance to exert his strength close up," said Gotch. "He was forced to use his power at arm's lengths, which greatly diminished it, of course."

Then, the magnaminous Gotch paid tribute to the fallen champ.

"Hackenschmidt is the most perfectly built man I have ever laid eyes on," the new world champ said. "Picture to yourself what you think a perfect physical man should be and you have Hack to a dot. He has not one superfluous ounce of meat on his bones; all muscle and sinew. He is certainly a magnificent specimen of physical manhood, a sight to look upon."

Yet, he was no match for the quick-thinking, quick-moving and supremely confident Gotch.

After Hackenschmidt, Gotch met all comers, crisscrossing the country, and never surrendered a single fall. His toughest American adversary was Dr. Benjamin Roller of Seattle, but it was, according to the account in the *Seattle Times*, another easy night.

Roller "was most constantly on the defensive from the smooth-moving Gotch, who glided from one hold to another with absolute grace and precision," wrote the Seattle reporter. After the rest period following the first fall, the two men returned to the center of the ring. Gotch "was smiling broadly, as usual, while Roller was mad clear through, and showed it in every action."

Touring Europe as the star of his play, Gotch drew crowds of 5,000 to 10,000 people in every city. He took time out to wrestle an English champion, and pinned him three times in less than three minutes.

"He is strong and moves like lightning. A man stands no chance against him," said the Englishman. "He is a master of ring craft. I have never met or read of a man like him. There is not an ounce of science in the ring that he does not know about. He uses a brainy science. In every move there is something in the background."

Back in the States, Gotch wrestled the great Bulgarian, Yussiff Mahmout, before another packed house in Chicago. Mahmout had quickly beaten every other American matman, but Gotch disposed of him with two falls in less than half an hour.

Edward Smith, the renown sports editor of the *Chicago American* newspaper, served as referee and wrote about Gotch's victory in glowing terms.

"Gotch's self possession was something wonderful to contemplate," wrote Smith. "I was flat on the canvas so as to get a good view under the Turk, and Gotch's face was turned toward me. He had a smile on his face and was scarcely breathing hard . . ."

Gotch's confidence wasn't confined to the wrestling arena, however. He took it with him wherever he went. Though he said he had never engaged in an all-out barroom fight, he was confident that he would emerge victorious if the situation ever occurred.

"Did you know that when the ju jitsu craze was speeding over the coast and there was talk of such an encounter, with everyone expressing dread of the Japanese that was then there demonstrating, $1,000 was posted on my behalf in a challenge to go into a room with a Jap and lock the door, the best man to unlock it? Well, that was so, and the Northwest papers of the day will sustain the statement. The challenge was never accepted. I never had a street or barroom fight in my life, but I'll bet $2,500 at any time that I will beat any man in America—and not barring Jeffries, either—at the style everything goes."

By 1915, Frank Gotch seemed to be sitting on top of the world. He had been undefeated world champion for seven years, raising wrestling to its brightest period ever. As a sport, it was more popular even than boxing, due in large part to Gotch's dynamic personality and good looks. He was said to have made the biggest fortune in the history of athletics at that time, and was married to his hometown sweetheart.

But a mysterious ailment struck him down. His body began to waste away, and he fought off sickness for two years. Finally, on Dec. 16, at just forty years of age, Frank Gotch died. The shocking news was carried on the front page of every newspaper in Iowa, and across much of the nation, as well. The tiny town of Humboldt swelled to three times its normal size as mourners came from all across the midwest. The governor of Iowa appeared at Gotch's funeral, and Teddy Roosevelt sent a telegram.

For the next thirty years, Gotch's name and photo appeared regularly in the leading physical culture magazines of the country. The words "world's greatest wrestler" nearly always accompanied them.

Nat Fleischer, the founder and publisher of the famous *Ring* magazine, and the person generally considered to be the world's foremost authority on wrestling before it turned theatrical, ranked the greatest wrestlers of all time in this order: Frank Gotch, George Hackenschmidt, Stanislaus Zbyszko, The Great Gama, and Ed "Strangler" Lewis. Gotch defeated Hackenschmidt in both their meetings, and also demolished Zbyszko, a giant of a man, winning the first fall in just six seconds with a hip toss. The Polish strongman had entered the Gotch match with 944 consecutive victories behind him.

The passing decades and the low esteem in which professional wrestling is held today have considerably diminished Gotch's reputation. Though at one time he was this country's most honored athlete, today is he hardly known at all outside small circles. He should be remembered, however, as being one of the toughest men in sports history. He should also be remembered as a champion who was always totally prepared, physically, and mentally, and was able to keep his overwhelming confidence in check, not allowing it to become openly arrogant. He was a champion who loved his sport deeply, and allowed himself to enjoy it as well as win at it.

In the boxing ring or on the wrestling mats, Dan Hodge was a winner. He won seven national wrestling titles, and was national Golden Gloves heavyweight boxing champion. He also was a pro athlete in both sports.

# DAN HODGE

# Wrestler-Boxer Extraordinaire

Boxing and wrestling have coexisted for thousands of years. The ancient Greeks used to practice an art called pankration, which was a combination of the two sports. The winners in these contests were exalted as no other athletes, becoming national heros on the highest levels.

In the early days of sport boxing in America, the lines drawn between boxing and wrestling were thin and easily crossed. When the legendary John L. Sullivan took the American bareknuckle prizefighting title from Paddy Ryan on February 7, 1882, he used wrestling techniques to help him win.

"Ryan could not match Sullivan's strength," according to Graham Houston in his book, *Superfists*. "He was thrown to the floor repeatedly in the wrestling that was permissable under prize ring rules."

Many of the early heavyweight boxing champions incorporated wrestling into their training routines. "Gentleman" Jim Corbett, the man who eventually dethroned Sullivan, and James J. Jeffries, champion from 1899 to 1904, enjoyed wrestling, and eventually became fast friends with Frank Gotch, the world professional wrestling champion. Jack Johnson, the first black man to wear sport's most coveted crown, wrestled competitively in Europe while he was the reigning king of boxers, and took pride in his wrestling ability.

Though boxing and wrestling are cousins in the world of sports, they are still distant kin and it is the rare athlete who is able to excel in both because the requirements are so different. Not only are the mechanics of the footwork and muscle development somewhat at odds, but the two sports are difficult to bring together in the mental preparation of a single athlete. While the boxer must have an unrestrained enthusiasm for punching and striking, the wrestler must have an equal predilection for pulling and grabbing.

In all of American history, no men ever achieved greater success in combining the sports than Paul Berlenbach and Dan Hodge.

Berlenbach, born in New York City in 1901, won the lightheavyweight (174 pounds) national AAU wrestling championships in 1920. Then, just two years later, he was national AAU lightheavyweight boxing champion. He turned to professional boxing in 1923, and in 1925 decisioned tough Jack Delaney for the world light-heavyweight championship. Delaney regained the title the following year, and Berlenbach retired from the prize ring in 1933, with a record of 37-8-3. He was elected to the Boxing Hall of Fame in 1971.

Hodge was the only man to ever match Berlenbach's tremendous feat of winning national championships in both boxing and wrestling. He stormed out of the Oklahoma plains in the 1950s to mold an athletic career that was amazing then, and is still amazing to wrestling followers today.

Hodge, like Berlenbach, began his career as a wrestler. He captured a state championship for Perry High School in Oklahoma, and then entered the United States Navy where he continued his mat career. He surprised even himself by making the 1952 Olympic team and, as a raw newcomer of just nineteen years of age, he placed fifth at the Olympic Games in Helsinki.

Hodge enrolled at the University of Oklahoma after his discharge from the service, and became the most feared collegiate wrestler of his era. By the time his remarkable college career was over, he had won all forty-six matches he had entered. He was a three-time conference champion, and won three NCAA ( National Collegiate Athletic Association) championships, the highest honor available to a collegiate matman. He was also selected the outstanding wrestler in the NCAA tournament in both his junior and senior years.

But perhaps the most impressive statistic of all was that he was never taken off his feet in any of his college matches. Amazingly, during his entire career, Hodge never surrendered a takedown—a common enough occurance in even a single match.

Hodge was also a pinner of outstanding impact. Only Bill Koll before him and Dan Gable after him would equal his penchant of pinning, which is the wrestler's equivalent to a knockout in boxing. Koll, who starred for three years at Iowa State Teacher's College in the 1940s, was known the width of the country for his ferocious pinning combinations, and so was Gable, who stampeded onto the collegiate scene at Iowa State in the 1960s.

At one point, Hodge flattened twenty-two straight opponents. His style was effective, if unspectacular. With his unbelievable wrist and hand power, he simply overwhelmed foe after foe, forcing them to their backs with a precision that was virtually unstoppable. Hodge pinned every man he met in the NCAA tournament as a junior, and pinned all but one his

**84**

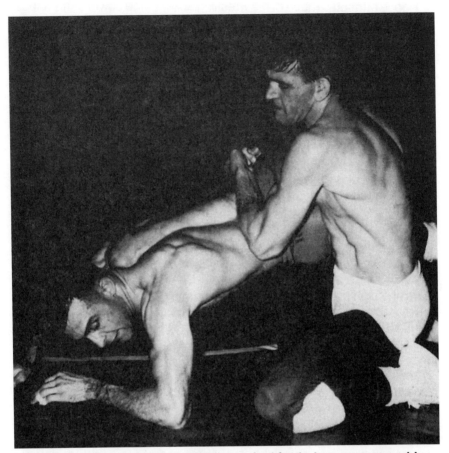

**A lean and mean Dan Hodge grimaces as he tries to turn an opponent to his back during their wrestling match in 1955. Hodge completed his collegiate career at the University of Oklahoma undefeated. He also won three NCAA championships at 177 pounds. Hodge was never taken down during his entire college career.**

senior year. The referee apparently took pity on John Dustin of Oregon State, because he stopped Hodge's legal hold each time he neared the pin and Dustin hollered out in agony.

To this day, Hodge is the only amateur wrestler ever to grace the cover of America's number one sports periodical, *Sports Illustrated*. Even the fabled Gable, though he was the subject of several in-depth articles by *Sports Illustrated*, never appeared on its cover. But there is Hodge, on the April 1, 1957 cover, clad in red tights, forcing the head of his opponent to the mat in his three-quarter nelson—a maneuver Hodge used with such frightening force that it was banned from the Olympic games after Hodge nearly broke the spine of a foreign matman.

Hodge attributes much of his wrestling ability to the power in his hands and wrists. It was the kind of power from which legends have sprouted, and it transformed him into something of a folk hero in the world of amateur wrestling. Just about any wrestler who has been around the sport long enough to cultivate a cauliflower ear knows at least one story about Hodge's Bunyonesque power.

"I once saw Hodge take a guy down with one hand," said Bob Dellinger, one of the nation's foremost authorities on amateur wrestling and now an official for USA Wrestling, the sport's governing body. "He grabbed the guy's wrist and the guy started to back away, trying to get his hand free. And then Dan snapped him, like you would a whip, back to the mat. I don't believe he ever had a close match in college."

Myron Roderick, a three-time NCAA champion at Oklahoma State University, which was the bitter mat rival of Hodge's Oklahoma team, was often a witness to Hodge's power.

"His strength was his greatest asset," said Roderick in the book *Two Guys Named Dan*. "After we made the Olympic team in 1956, we walked into a hardware store and asked the manager if he had a strong pair of pliers and Dan squeezed them and popped the bolt between the halves. The manager said it must have been a weak pair and gave us another pair and Dan proceeded to do the same thing. As long as I have been in wrestling Dan Hodge has the most strength in his hands and arms of anyone I have ever seen . . ."

Another Oklahoma matman who could vouch for Hodge's fantastic displays of hand power was Grady Peninger, later a successful coach at Michigan State University.

"Dan Hodge was as strong as nine acres of garlic," said Peninger. "The tales about him crushing apples with his hands and bending the handles off a pair of pliers are certainly not over exaggerated. Pound-for-pound, he is the strongest wrestler I have ever witnessed. Sometimes his opponents would make the mistake of resisting when Dan put on a three-quarter nelson; you can't imagine the sounds that emitted from the spine as Dan gradually bent the head under. I am sure that he gave chiropractors more business than any past or present amateur wrestler."

Hodge says his strength is a gift from God. He claims to have two tendons controlling each finger, while the normal person has just one. At any rate, what Hodge can do with his hands is awe-inspiring. He delights in "funning" with fans, pulling his index finger far to one side, then letting it snap back into place with a snapping sound similar to someone cracking his knuckles. He can make a fist, then rub his fingers together, making a noise like twigs crackling. And when he reaches to shake another man's hand, it takes courage for the other man not to withdraw it. Hodge can assert so much pressure in a simple handshake that he can force another man to his knees.

**Dan Hodge, one of the greatest amateur wrestlers of all time and for many years a top professional star, displays his amazing hand strength by crushing an apple into instant applesauce. Hodge is also noted for his ability to snap the handles off a pair of pliers merely by exerting the tremendous strength of his hands.**

"Shaking hands with Dan is like putting your hands between two boards," said Jon Marks, a 280-pounder who first met Hodge in 1976. "There's just no give to his hands at all."

It was that kind of reputation that preceded Hodge in his wrestling meets in America. In 1956, he captured a national AAU freestyle championship by pinning all six men he faced. He then entered his first-ever Greco-Roman (above-the-waist-holds only), and won that championship with four straight pins. A week earlier, he had won his second straight NCAA title with four pins. In just a little over a week's time, Hodge had won three national titles against America's best, wrestling fourteen matches and scoring fourteen pins!

And yet the Oklahoma dynamo had to settle for a silver medal in the 1956 Olympics in Melbourne. It remains, to this day, one of the biggest disappointments in his life. Hodge began the competition with three pins and a lop-sided decision. Then, in his fifth match, he constructed a large lead over his Bulgarian foe. With two seconds remaining in the second period, Hodge was called for a pin because he rolled through a move on his shoulders, without the Bulgarian wrestler actually even touching him. The Bulgarian was given the highly controversial victory and wound up with the gold medal. Hodge came back to pin the wrestler from the Soviet Union in such a stunning fashion that his hold, the three-quarter nelson, was outlawed for being too vicious.

"He is one of the strongest men ever to set foot on a mat and was directly responsible for the three-quarter nelson being ruled ineligible in international competition," said Wayne Baughman, an Olympain both as a wrestler and a coach. "He was applying the hold with such pressure in the Olympics that it was said you could hear him snapping spines in the second row."

Years later, an Australian wrestling coach visiting in America said the Hodge match with the Bulgarian was one of the worst cases of injustice he had ever seen in international sports.

When Hodge returned to America after the 1956 Olympics, he won his third straight NCAA title, graduated from college and was on the verge of retiring from sports. It was then he decided to give boxing a twirl.

"I had always been interested in boxing," said Hodge. "I kind of thought I'd do okay, but then I really wasn't sure. It's a big transition switching from wrestling to boxing. In wrestling, you work to keep your muscles tight so that you can wrestle with a lot of squeezing-type power. But in boxing you have to keep your muscles loose and relaxed, so that you can strike at a moment's notice.

"Then, the footwork is a little different, too. Though I generally wrestled with both feet squared off, in boxing I had to lead with one foot in front of the other."

Whatever transition was to be made, Hodge did it swiftly and convincingly. He knocked his first opponent down nine times in the first round and finished him off early in the second. It was to be the first of seventeen straight victories.

At the Golden Gloves Tournament of Champions in Chicago in 1960,

Hodge flattened his finals foe in the opening round. His showing brought flowing words of praise from *Chicago Tribune* sportswriter Maurice Shelvin.

"It isn't every day that Chicago fight fans have a chance to see a world champion in the making but here they'll have that opportunity. Some of those who saw Dan Hodge in action during the Tournament of Champions last week see in the 25-year-old another Rocky Marciano," wrote Shelvin.

"Hodge, of Irish-German parentage, is not only built on Marciano's lines (but has) the same slashing manner of throwing punches that characterized Rocky's attack in his heyday . . ."

When Hodge knocked out a veteran slugger two weeks later in the final of the Western Championship, Shelvin labelled it "one of the greatest heavyweight bouts in the history of the Golden Gloves."

Winning the Western title qualified Hodge to meet the Eastern champion, Fred Hood, in New York City, where the winner would be declared national champion. Hood, a crafty veteran, knocked Hodge to the canvas twice in the opening round, but Hodge overwhelmed him in the second round after just two minutes and twenty-three seconds had elapsed. The crowd of 11,500 gave Hodge a five-minute standing ovation for his knockout victory.

Hodge had joined Berlenbach in one of the rarest doubles in sports history. And he was contemplating what might have led to the most remarkable athletic feat of all time—trying to make the 1960 Olympic team in three sports: freestyle wrestling, Greco-Roman wrestling and boxing. But he had a family to think about and decided to turn professional. As a pro boxer, he was 8-2, losing his last fight when he was horribly overmatched against world-ranking heavyweight Nino Valdes. Hodge was cut to ribbons, but was never knocked off his feet.

Disappointed in the money he was receiving, Hodge gave up boxing and turned to professional wrestling. For many years he was one of the most popular professional wrestlers in the southern half of the United States and in Japan, wrestling in main events and drawing large crowds. But even in the kooky world of professional wrestling, Hodge managed to compete with dignity. "I never changed my name, moved out of town or wore a mask," said Hodge simply. "People can say pro wrestling is phoney, but I wish they would pay some of my phoney doctor bills." Hodge retired from wrestling in the late 1970s after a number of serious injuries, which included a broken neck suffered in an auto accident. Another injury that Hodge sustained resulted in the removal of a portion of his stomach, an operation which left a long scar across his midsection.

But the years of pro wrestling also left Hodge with a vast knowledge of submission and choke holds left over from the earlier days of professional wrestling.

Verne Gagne, a two-time NCAA champion at the University of Minnesota, gave up professional football for the bigger money available in pro wrestling and became a grappling superstar in the 1950s. Gagne, like Hodge, was one of the most knowledgeable and scientific of wrestlers, having had an extensive background in amateur sport to draw on.

"The thing about professional wrestling is the wealth of knowledge that is being lost," said Gagne once. "The old pros knew all kinds of arm locks, arm bars and strangle-type holds, really effective stuff. But as the years slip by, those guys die, and lots of the knowledge doesn't get passed on." Today Hodge knows as much about wrestling as any man alive, with the possible exception of men like Gagne, Pat O'Connor and Lou Thesz. He once demonstrated the fabled sleeper hold in his living room, catching a non-believer in the maneuver and instantly putting him to sleep.

"I didn't know that the sleeper was a real hold," the victim, who happened to be a journalist, said later. "I had seen it used a dozen times, but always deep down thought it was hokey. When I mentioned that to Dan, he laughed and asked if he could put one on me. Well, he did, and I felt myself passing out immediately. I reached back to tap him on the shoulder to let go, and the next hing I knew I was lying on the floor looking up at a group of people. They were all staring down at me, and I jumped right up. I asked Dan's wife, Dolores, how long I was on the floor, and she said about twenty seconds . . ."

Whatever professional wrestling has or has not become, it is not an activity for the weak of body, or the weak of spirit. It is a demanding, gruelling profession that requires constant travel, long nights, a sturdy body and a knowledge of wrestling techniques and fundamentals. The show element came in shortly after the death of the one and only Frank Gotch in 1917, when the sport hit a long dry spell.

In Gotch's period, "There were a few of the gimmicks that were to characterize the post-war era," wrote Graeme Kent in his book, *A Pictorial History of Wrestling*, "and to modern eyes the bouts engaged in by Gotch and his contemporaries might sometimes have seemed slow and ponderous. But they were tough and rugged—and honest. No breath of suspicion ever attached itself to Frank Gotch."

Dan Hodge actually belonged to both worlds. He was a throwback to the days of Gotch, and would have fared extremely well in that competition. He had many characteristics in common with Gotch—fabulous conditioning, a fierce pride, a wide knowledge of holds, great speed and an overwhelming confidence in himself.

Hodge isn't bashful when it comes to offering his opinion on the relative merits of boxing and wrestling. "It all depends on the men, rather than the styles," said Hodge after thinking the situation over. "But in most cases I'd have to go with the wrestler. I know I'd lots rather know wrestling as a self defense than boxing. How many times have you ever seen anyone take someone out with one or two clean punches? Not very often. Usually, there are a few punches thrown, and the two men clinch or grab

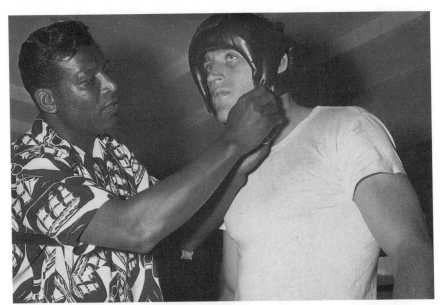

**Dan Hodge, one of only two men to ever win national championships in both boxing and wrestling, has his headgear adjusted by the legendary Sugar Ray Robinson prior to a 1960 workout.**

one another. When that happens the wrestler has a decided advantage. If he can weather the first couple of punches, he should be in his home territory, and should have an excellent chance of winning."

There have been a number of instances where a wrestler has met a boxer in a mixed match. One of the most famous came in 1910, and pitted world class athletes in their own environment. Farmer Burns, who was Gotch's trainer, was in Reno, Nevada in 1910 helping former heavyweight boxing champion Jim Jeffries in his comeback against titleholder Jack Johnson. Burns and Billy Papke, middleweight boxing champion, fell to arguing and bet $1,000 on the outcome of a match between them. Both men weighed around 170 pounds, and Burns pinned the boxer in eighteen seconds.

In 1935, former mat champ Ray Steele and boxer Kingfish Levinsky squared off. Levinsky tagged Steele with two quick punches, but the matman shrugged them off and took the boxer down, pinning him in less than a minute. Jack Dempsey, one of the greatest boxing champs of all time, knocked out a series of wrestlers in the 1930s, but the wrestlers all entered the ring with boxing gloves and fought under boxing rules, not mixed rules.

When it comes to the relative merits of boxing and wrestling, Dan Hodge is as knowledgeable as anybody, because he speaks from the rarest of vantage points. In all of American sports history, only he and Paul Berlenbach ever reached the summit in both sports.

**Dan Gable, one of the greatest collegiate athletes of all time, strikes a pose during his glory days at Iowa State University. Gable won 180 consecutive high school and college wrestling matches and was called "The Machine" for his methodical destruction of opponents. He is regarded as the greatest pinner in wrestling history.**

# DAN GABLE

# Total Commitment And Dedication

One way to measure a champion is by the sacrifice he has made to be a champion. If one accepts that criteria, then no champion in any sport can surpass the accomplishments of Dan Gable. Surely no athlete who ever lived gave more of himself in pursuit of excellence than Gable. Ask any wrestler in America, or just about any wrestler in the Soviet Union, where amateur wrestling is far more appreciated.

"All Soviet wrestling fans remember Dan Gable," said Ivan Yarygan, 1972 and 1976 Olympic champion, when touring the United States as coach of the Soviet Union team in 1983. "He was the greatest American wrestler I ever saw. Soviet fans appreciate him yet today."

Gable's march to the Olympic gold medal in 1972 in Munich was astounding. He entered the regional trials in Iowa City, Iowa, and won all six matches by pin, giving up a total of one point. He then advanced to the final trials and won seven more matches, giving up just one more point. With the top two competitors selected at each weight, additional tryouts were set up. Gable defeated Lloyd Keaser, who was to be world champion just one year later, 22-0 and 11-0.

Then Gable was in the Olympics. Despite two bad knees—one that would demand surgery shortly after his return to America—and a gash suffered over his eye in the first match (a cut that would require seven stitches), Gable beat all six foes—without surrendering a single point.

Dan Gable had earned his Olympic gold medal, and the path had been strewn with stunned victims. Beginning in Iowa City and continuing through the Games, Gable took to the mat twenty-one times and gave up a total of two points. That would be comparable to Nolan Ryan pitching twenty-one straight games, and giving up just two hits. It was an unbelievable performance. Yet the Gable legend was full of such performances.

Gable began his athletic career as a skinny red-headed kid in Waterloo, Iowa. As a youngster, he earned a state championship in swimming, was the quarterback of an undefeated junior high school football team, and was a pretty fair baseball player on the Little League level. Entering the tenth grade, and high school, Gable analyzed his situation and made a choice. He knew he could be a respectable athlete in several different sports, or try to excel in one. He chose the latter route, and wrestling.

"I think courage has many faces," wrote Frank Gifford in his book, *Courage.* "Dan Gable's single-minded assault on a dream set as a teenager is, to me, heroic. To dedicate one's mind, body and heart to an almost unreachable goal every day of every year from adolesence through high school, college, and two years further requires an extraordinary intensity of purpose and discipline. To push one's body to the limit of endurance and then beyond, to deny oneself normal pleasures while all around are enjoying those pleasures, to perservere under gruelling competition is, to me, a rare facet of courage. Dan Gable's courage."

The first demonstration of the courage Gifford referred to came during Gable's sophomore year of wrestling at Waterloo West High School. Electing to compete in the 95-pound weight class, Gable trimmed his weight from 127 pounds to 95 pounds. It was a painful sacrifice that would, in later years, cause Gable to reevaluate weight cutting, one of the most unpopular aspects of amateur wrestling. But the young dynamo was, nonetheless, very successful as a high school sophomore. He racked up 20 straight wins, and won the Iowa high school state championship. Gable moved up a weight class each of the next two years, and finished high school with three state championships and a 64-0 record.

Enrolling at Iowa State University, Gable continued his mat odyssey. He entered the tough Midlands Tournament (considered America's finest mat meet because post-college as well as college wrestlers are eligible) and stunned the wrestling world by defeating two national champions, Don Behm and Massaki Hatta, claiming the title at 130 pounds. It was the beginning of a remarkable string. Gable would eventually wrestle in six Midlands, compiling six championships and a 31-0 record. He would also be named the meet's outstanding wrestler on five of those six occasions.

In addition, Gable was building another remarkable string. Counting high school and college competition, Gable racked up 180 straight wins—an achievement that landed him in the *Guinness Book of Records.* Gable also began to attract attention to amateur wrestling like never before. Huge crowds showed up to watch him compete, and national magazines began to take notice.

*Sports Illustrated* dubbed him "Superwrestler" before his junior year at Iowa State University was over, calling him "the most exciting wrestler since Dan Hodge came out of Oklahoma in 1955." They continued, "For openers, he has won 139 straight bouts in nearly six years of high school and college. But what sets Gable apart is how he wins, which is by pinning

**94**

his opponent's shoulders to the mat rather than straining to a decision."

*Amateur Wrestling News*, which is considered the Bible of the amateur wrestling world, labelled Gable "the greatest pinner in college history." And no wonder. His record in college was built around the pin.

As a junior, Gable defeated 28 straight foes, 26 by pin. The two men he didn't pin were defeated by scores of 25-6 and 12-1. During his entire college career, Gable scored 85 pins in 120 matches.

But still, the most talked-about aspect of Gable's career was his devotion to training. He was called a wild man by some, a fanatic by others. In wrestling circles his name was synonymous with dedication.

"Since graduating from high school, Gable has not taken a break from wrestling," reported *Sports Illustrated*. "In fact, he is called The Machine. During the past 32 months, he has spent 3,000 hours training and wrestling, and he concedes that his interest in the sport borders on the obsession."

Gable stampeded through the wrestling world like a runaway tornado. And then the unthinkable happened. After 180 straight matches, wrestling in his very last collegiate match, Superwrestler was beaten. Larry Owings, a sophomore from the University of Washington, sent shock waves through the mat world with a 13-11 victory over Gable in the finals of the NCAA tournament in 1970 at Northwestern University.

Some predicted Gable would fall apart under the pressure and pain of his first loss, but just two weeks later Gable won a national freestyle tournament and was on his way again. He stormed through tournament after tournament, piling up more titles. The living room of his parents' home began to look like a department store specializing in trophies, plaques and silver trays.

Gable was heading toward the Olympics, non-stop. Working out twice and sometimes three times a day, every day, he honed his body to a condition that was unparalleled in sports.

"He feels pain just like anyone else and he gets tired just like anyone," said Jon Marks, one of his closest friends, "but the difference is Dan just never submits to it. He doesn't quit, ever . . ."

He ran mile after mile in the solitude of the early morning or late at night. Once, when he and friends were watching the Soviet basketball team play on television, the others left at the game's conclusion to drink some beer. Gable, motivated by the thought of the Soviets, put on his sweats and took off running, at 11 p.m.

When Gable first hit the Soviet Union, he surprised, then shocked, the world's best wrestlers. He won the 149-pound class at the Tblisi meet, one of the toughest in the world, was named the outstanding wrestler, and was presented with a bear cloak and a huge vase. At the banquet that night, the Soviet coach said his goal for 1972 was to find a wrestler who could defeat Gable at the Olympics. He was the first American to ever shake up the Russians in such a manner.

**Showing an expression of disgust, wrestler Dan Gable looks to the side of the mat after suffering a gash over his eye in the opening match of the 1972 Olympics. Gable was injured by a head butt from his Yugoslav foe, but scored a pin after the injury. Gable's gash required seven stitches, but he won the gold medal in the 149-pound class without surrendering a single point in his six bouts. (Wide World Photos)**

Gable won the world championship in 1971, and became the favorite for the Olympic title. Despite his knees and eye gash, he did all that was expected of him.

Both Ben and John Peterson, gold and silver medalists in 1972 at 198 pounds and 180 pounds, respectively, said they owed much of their success to Gable. He was the team's leader, and inspiration.

"Watching Gable makes us understand we can do more," said J. Robinson, a member of the 1972 Olympic team and now an assistant coach for Gable at the University of Iowa. "We all work hard; you don't qualify for the Olympics unless you do. But Gable makes us realize we're capable of giving more."

"He opened up a whole new era for athletes, really," said Gary Kurdelmeier, who coached the University of Iowa to its first two NCAA team titles, and hired Gable as his assistant in 1972. "Gable is a trendsetter. Nobody ever worked as hard as he did to reach the top. Now others have a chance to emulate that, if they will."

"I personally feel Dan Gable and his career moved wrestling through a psychological barrier similar to the four-minute mile in track," said Ken Kraft, assistant athletic director at Northwestern University, and for many years the color man on ABC's "Wide World of Sports" wrestling reports. "By that I mean his gargantuan work load was so well covered by the media that young wrestlers in huge numbers began to accept what they should do to become a success.

"We all recognized Dan's almost unbelievable high school and college record. All areas of interest need a hero that can be appreciated by the masses. Dan Gable is that man in wrestling."

The Olympic exposure was tremendous for both Gable and wrestling. ABC followed his every move, and Chris Schenkel declared that he might be the best conditioned athlete in the world.

Returning home, Gable was invited to appear on such television shows as "To Tell the Truth," "Dick Cavett" and "The Superstars." Feature articles appeared on him and his training in *Esquire* magazine (written by John Irving, of "Garp" fame), *The Fighters,* and others. An aspiring actress, telling a reporter from *TV Guide* how hard she worked to make it to the top of her profession, compared herself to Gable in terms of dedication.

When Gable finally decided to hang up his knee pads, he had compiled the amazing record of 305 wins and seven defeats. After twelve long years of wrestling, against the best competition on a national and world level, he had lost just seven times. Among his many victims were world champions and national champions. Many of them were not just outscored, but pinned by Gable.

Gable's next challenge was coaching, and he responded with the same dedication that had underscored his wrestling. Kurdelmeier turned over the head coaching job to Gable after the two served as a team for just four years, and Gable mowed through the coaching ranks in the

**Dan Gable works on a foe during the 1972 Olympics in Munich. Gable's head is bandaged because of the cut suffered during the match with his Yugoslav opponent.**

same fashion he had the grappling world. After seven years of Gable's coaching, the University of Iowa had won seven straight Big Ten Conference championships and six NCAA trophies. Gable's record of 122-5-2 is one of the very best in college history, in any sport. Against teams in the Big Ten, the conference Iowa competes in, Gable's record was 46-0 after the 1983 season.

At the NCAA tournament in March of 1983, Gable's Hawkeyes shattered the team scoring record with 155 points. Oklahoma State, the proud owner of twenty-seven team championships since the sport began NCAA competition in 1928, set a school record of 102 points—but still trailed Iowa by 53 points.

No man in American history can match Gable's impact on amateur wrestling. And the key to all of his successes is his single-minded pursuit of excellence—his commitment and dedication.

"I think the thing that impressed me more than anything else about Dan is that he felt he should never have a bad night, either in workouts or competition," said Bob Siddens, who coached Gable in high school. "This includes many hundreds and thousands of workouts, and the impression came about because he has been the only wrestler I have had in the past twenty-five plus years who was that way. I felt that Dan always did the best he possibly could. Most other athletes tend to believe they naturally will have a letdown in their workouts occasionally, but Dan never felt this way."

It showed. Anyone who ever stepped onto a mat to wrestle with Gable, either in a workout session or in competition, had to be prepared to go all out. It was either that or be destroyed. Gable never coasted in any workout during his competitive years.

"The individuals who really become champions are the ones who know that it takes considerable extra effort, substantially more than what the average wrestler is willing to expend," said Gable. "The Olympic-quality wrestler is the one who, in addition to his regular practice, works out every morning, who goes out and runs at least two to three miles before classes. He is the one who sets up a program of weight-lifting for himself and follows it year around.

"It's the attitude of a champion that sets him apart from others and helps him become a champion."

Gable was a hard worker all through high school, very seldom dating or socializing. Though popular, he preferred the life of a recluse, working out while others partied. The philosophy continued through the Olympics, but really gathered steam when he entered college.

"I thought that I was so far behind some of the other wrestlers in actual ability that the only way I could catch them was to work two and three times as hard as they did," said Gable. "I made up my mind that I would be the first one in the wrestling room and the last one to leave; that I would work out more than anyone else and with anyone that was available."

Size never mattered to Gable when selecting a workout partner. Actually, he preferred to wrestle with someone twenty or thirty pounds heavier, as it soon became apparent that he was unable to get a good match from anyone even close to his weight.

John Peterson, a gold medal winner in the 1976 Olympics two weights above Gable (180 pounds for John, 149 for Gable), admitted at one point during the 1977 season that he felt he had never even broken even with Gable in a workout session. Other wrestlers who are national champs at much higher weights have also been handled easily by Gable.

"That's one of the most amazing aspects of Dan," said Mark Johnson, a member of the 1980 Olympic team in the 198-pound class who has also

# The Des Moines Register *Peach*

THURSDAY, AUGUST 31, 1972 ★★★★★ 1-S

## U.S. Cagers Topple Brazil, 61-54; Spitz Goes After 2 More Medals---

# GABLE WITHIN GRASP OF GOLD

### FORMER IOWAN HEADS U.S. CONTINGENT---

## Buck Busy at Games

**Maury White** of the OLYMPICS

Crushing Victory for Chris

### ONLY RUSSIAN IN DAN'S WAY —MEET TODAY

Petersons, Taylor Gain on Mat

### WOOD ERROR LETS BOSTON TOP SOX, 4-2

Loss Drops Chicago 1½ Games Back

## Top-Seeded Smith Beats Teen in Fierce Struggle

The Scoreboard

---

# The Des Moines Register *Peach*

TUESDAY, AUGUST 29, 1972 ★★★★★ 1-S

## Taylor Rebounds From First-Round Mixup; Russians' Mat Streak to 20---

# GABLE WHIPS OLYMPIC FOE, 20-0

### 2 Petersons Also Gain

### IOWAN IN CHARGE OF 'WHAT HAVE YOU'---

## Helmick at Helm of Polo Chances

**Maury White** of the OLYMPICS

The Scoreboard
National League
Standings

### SPITZ CRACKS WORLD MARK, WINS 2 GOLDS

Micki King Nails Diving Crown

By Will Grimsley

### 'NEVER-QUIT' SOX TOPPLE BOSTON, 6-4

Andrews' 5 RBIs Rip Ex-Mates

gained a national reputation in weightlifting and body-building. "The first time I worked out with Dan I weighed a lot more and felt I was too strong for him. But I soon found out that size and strength doesn't make any difference when you wrestle Dan Gable. He just goes through it like it's not even there."

One of the many secrets to Gable's fantastic success is mat position. It's nearly impossible, as most of the world found out in 1972, to score on Gable because it's so difficult to catch him out of position. And the reason Gable has such extraordinary mat position is because of his endless workouts. It's nearly impossible to put him in a situation he hasn't already faced in a practice situation and, therefore, one in which he is susceptible to being scored upon.

Gable also used the concept of visualization.

"I won the state title a hundred, no a thousand times in my basement before I ever won it for real," said Gable. "When I'd get tired and wanted to stop working out, I'd wonder what my opponent was doing. I'd wonder if he was still working out, and I'd try to visualize that. Then when I could almost see him working out, I'd push myself harder and harder.

"Soon everyone knew how hard I was working; the guys on my team knew it, and my opponents, too. And when I got on the mat for real, they got scared. I had that mental edge."

Like Muhammad Ali, Gable played havoc with the mental outlook of his opponents. They knew when they faced Gable they were going to wrestle the full time—every second. There was no resting, no respite. Gable asked no quarter and offered none. He systematically wore wrestlers down physically, and then began to tear them down mentally. Most of his pins came late in the match, when he had already fashioned huge leads and the other matmen were exhausted.

"You can't go wrong if you're always on the move," said Gable after the Olympics. "Sometimes in practice I used to get real tired. Sometimes I'm afraid that I can't finish some move . . . but I keep driving and pushing anyway. It becomes a mental attitude, then, to never give up, to never quit."

Wrestling is, according to Gable, mostly mental once you reach a certain level of skill. But, he maintains, for a wrestler to be prepared mentally he must have paid the price physically.

"Yeah, I think wrestling is more mental than physical," he said. "People have a tendency to hold back. The only reason they don't do what they are capable of is because they are restrained mentally. They think that they are not prepared to go all out.

"I imagine there are wrestlers who have more natural shape than I do, but I don't think they've put as much into their training as I have."

That's confidence, another large factor in Gable's success.

"Besides knowing all the moves in wrestling, you must know that you know them—in other words, you must have confidence in yourself," said

**Intensity was one of the key ingredients to the success of Dan Gable, the wrestler, and it continues to be a key to Gable, the coach. Here, Gable (left) listens as University of Iowa assistant coach J. Robinson provides instruction to one of the Hawkeye wrestlers prior to a big match in 1983. (Photo by John McIvor)**

Gable. "I work hard at making my team tougher by requiring them to expend an 'extra effort' during practice sessions. By having them work particularly hard at practice, we are not only strengthening them physically but toughening them mentally . . .

"When I observe wrestlers walking onto the mat I know who is going to win—the one who is confident. There is only one legitimate way to have a lot of confidence—to be tough mentally, be prepared technically, and be in superior condition."

Gable was in a constant pursuit of perfection as a wrestler, and no American wrestler ever came closer. His high school and college combined record of 180-1, and his Olympic performance was perfect. He simply made no mistakes in marching to the title.

Now he strives for the same perfection as a coach.

"I look at our team on an individual basis," said Gable. "I tell each wrestler that the best thing he can do for the team is not to worry about how someone else will do, but be prepared to win himself. Then the other wrestlers can worry only about their matches. If everyone takes care of themselves, we can do okay."

Since Gable's arrival at the University of Iowa, the city has become a Mecca for wrestlers who aspire to be nationally or internationally prominent. "It's the only place to be in America if you want to be the best," said one young wrestler. "Everyone knows Gable is the greatest ever, and that he knows the most about wrestling of anyone in this country. The records prove that over and over."

Gable has come to stand for a number of things in today's wrestling society. He was the best wrestler in American amateur history, and is now the best coach. He represents victory in its most idealized form. And he also stands for dedication and commitment.

"I knew of no sport where a champion hasn't begun with talent and then concentrated on honing it," wrote Gifford. "Gable is perhaps the lone exception. His natural abilities are minimal. All he had was a desire to be the world's best wrestler."

**Wayne Baughman, coach of the United States Olympic team in 1976, gestures at the side of the match during an important bout. Baughman, an officer in the United States Air Force, has coached and competed in most of the world's top wrestling meets.**

# WAYNE BAUGHMAN

# Using Negative Reinforcement

Dan Gable, wrestler extraordinaire, sits on the side of a mat, his face etched in a hard, fixed expression. Sweat runs down him in rivers. The man who once won 180 straight high school and college matches, and went through the Olympics without a single point scored on him, is talking about his great love, his consuming passion.

"My kids win because wrestling is important to them and they're fighters," he says, his words measured. "They win because of attitude more than anything else. Wrestling is a very mental sport and it's a scary sport. Really, you're almost in a fight out there . . ."

Those are words that Major Wayne Baughman can easily identify with. Baughman lives over five hundred miles from Gable's Iowa City, Iowa home, serving as the wrestling coach at the United States Air Force Academy in Colorado Springs, Colorado. Philosophically, however, he resides next door to Gable. In fact, they may share the very same house.

Baughman's career borders on the fantastic. Though he has not gained near as much fame as Gable, Baughman has actually earned more national wrestling titles. In fact, in his long and victory-splashed career, Baughman has won more national championships than any other man in American amateur history.

For nearly three decades, wrestling has been a way of life for Baughman. In fact, it has been the way of life. He has competed in twenty-five national tournaments, and has, incredibly, never placed lower than third in any of them. His performance includes sixteen first places, seven seconds and two thirds. He has won national championships in every major style of wrestling—collegiate or folkstyle (NCAA), freestyle (Amateur Athletic Union—or AAU), Greco-Roman (above-the-waist only holds) and sombo. The latter is Russian judo, and combines freestyle wrestling with judo, permitting submission holds. It is not a sport for the faint of heart.

Even more amazingly, Baughman has placed in world competition in all three major international styles of combat—freestyle wrestling, Greco-Roman wrestling and sombo. It's a record that exposes not only Baughman's versatility, but his toughness as well.

Baughman has not, however, limited his activities to participation on the mats. He has not only competed in the Olympics and world games, but he has instructed at them. He has served as head coach of United States wrestling teams that have competed in three world championships, and of the American team that competed in the 1976 Olympics in Montreal. He has been matside at many of the most important wrestling tournaments in the world, absorbing information as he instructed. He was named coach of the year by the AAU, and is already a member of both national wrestling halls of fame.

Despite all his accomplishments, Baughman is a relatively young man. He was born in January of 1941. Today, at age forty two, he is lean, muscular and ramrod straight, giving the impression of a coiled spring— a disciplined warrior ready for action. He looks like what he is—a great competitor in one of man's most rugged and demanding sports, and an officer in the world's finest air force. He is a man who commands respect. But it was not always so. In fact, it was his determination to gain respect that started Baughman on his wrestling odyssey. The desire for respect, and, as Baughman himself puts it, negative motivation.

"There is nothing mystical about the emotional side of sport," wrote Thomas Tutko, in *Sports Psyching*. "Such matters can be defined and dealt with in deliberate, rational ways. Obviously, you can't control the weather or field conditions. You can't change luck and you can't change the other players (much). But you can be in control of yourself and your emotions—and thereby play your own game."

Baughman was able to assess his emotions, understand them, and use them as a motivational factor in his athletic pursuits.

"I think most people who excel, particularly in wrestling, are often reacting to a negative personality trait," said Baughman in his straightforward manner. "And I think it's true in the martial arts too. In my own particular case, I had a lot of resentment, hostility; I didn't particularly like myself or anyone else . . . I wanted to get an education, to prove to all the people at my high school that I wasn't the bum that they thought I was. That was my major motivation."

Tutko addressed himself to this very situation later on in his book:

"We are all social animals with the need to be liked and respected, to both fit in with others and yet to stand out sufficiently so that our individual worth is recognized. We are a mix of many emotions and drives, and many of them are in conflict with one another. On the game field, that conflict can turn to combat . . . there is always the feeling when you play

**Wayne Baughman (top) applies a tough ride on an Iowa State University opponent. Baughman, wrestling for the University of Oklahoma, was NCAA champion in 1962 in the 191-pound weight division.**

that you are somehow being tested, being judged as a person as well as a player."

Some athletes welcome that opportunity to be judged on the athletic field, for they know that is where they can scale the heights.

Baughman not only earned athletic honors, he also earned respect in the classroom. He holds a bachelor of science degree in education from the University of Oklahoma, and a master of arts degree from the University of Denver. At the Air Force Academy, he is an associate professor of physical education.

Wrestling practices at John Marshall High School in Oklahoma City, under coach Virgil Milliron, were tough, demanding, productive and rewarding. But only for those who had a constitution strong enough to survive and grow, both physically and emotionally. Two of Milliron's best students were Baughman and, later, Wayne Wells, who became an NCAA champion at the University of Oklahoma and then earned a gold medal in the 1972 Olympics.

Said Baughman, "I was taught that you should go out to pin your opponent or defeat him as soundly as possible but to never humiliate or unnecessarily intimidate your opponent—to respect your opponent and not do anything to embarrass him. I learned that respect could be earned even in defeat or lost in victory if one did not demonstrate respect for his opponent.

"We had that philosophy in both competition and in the workout room. Coach Milliron told us that that attitude would make us better, and our opponent better, too. Confidence, pride, respect—anything less than that—than a total commitment—is not fair to either oneself or his opponent. It's a lesson that I have never forgotten."

Although Baughman never won a state high school championship in Oklahoma—he had to settle for third in the state meet as a senior—he captured the eyes of Tommy Evans and Port Robertson, the coaches at the University of Oklahoma and two of the sport's best at taking tough, raw kids with heart and molding them into national champions. Robertson had done just that some years earlier with an Oklahoma prep named Dan Hodge and Tommy Evans was carrying on the tradition.

It didn't take Robertson and Evans long to realize that in Baughman they had a diamond in the rough. From Port Robertson Baughman learned "win or lose, be confident when you walk off the mat that if it had been a street fight you would have won"—which Baughman could certainly relate to since the reason he had originally gotten involved in wrestling was because he was kicked off the basketball team for fighting.

He also learned the philosophy from his coaches, "to go out to pin and totally dominate an opponent and not to worry about the score, as the score would take care of itself." That philosophy worked well, except for seven times in his collegiate career (54-7 record), and was also particularly appropriate and beneficial in his later international wrestling career.

Years after their collegiate association had ended, Robertson wrote that he had known "many outstanding wrestlers over the years, but none who were more dedicated or gave a greater effort than Wayne." Both Robertson (1960) and Evans (1968) were U.S. Olympic freestyle wrestling team coaches.

Baughman was one of the first to recognize that, as a wrestler, he had limitations. He was not as fluid or as slick or as skilled as many that he would compete against in the years ahead. But he made up for those shortcomings by his burning desire to succeed—a desire fed and nurtured by negative reinforcement and a mental toughness that seldom deserted him. If others would excel with grace, he would excel with guts.

"Mental preparation is the one thing that separates the Olympic athlete—or the super athlete—from just the good athlete," said Baughman. "Very definitely, at the highest level of competition, the mental and emotional level is the most important aspect of winning, because the athletes are, or should be, fairly equal on a physical level.

"Mental preparation is very, very important. And, it's very difficult to separate the mental, physical, psychological and emotional areas of competition. But I do think that total concentration of effort—mental, physical and emotional—makes the difference."

Baughman uses his own career to bring the point home in dramatic fashion.

"When I started slipping and going downhill as a competitor is when I quit doing it mentally," he said. "I think I was still there physically . . . maybe even better than ever. But any time I lost that mental edge, that concentration . . . well, I was in trouble."

That didn't happen often. The record book is proof of that. But when he did lose the mental edge, he found the results far from satisfying.

In the 1968 Olympics when wrestling an opponent from the Soviet Union, a country that consistently produces the best amateur wrestlers in the world, Baughman found himself leading the defending world champion by a 3-0 score. The match was close to being over; eight and one half minutes had expired, with only thirty seconds remaining to be contested. Baughman was nearly home free, with a victory that he would cherish the rest of his life. Instead, the roof caved in.

"I was ahead, and I lost respect for my opponent," said Baughman, sadly reflecting on the moment. "He had quit, I really felt that. And that's why I lost respect. Then I relaxed on the side of the mat when he threw a sloppy move. Instead of stepping off that mat, which was acceptable under those rules, I stayed in there and fought it (the move). It was a mental breakdown that cost me.

"Losing respect for an opponent, relaxing on the mat edge toward the end of a period, not using the rules in one's favor—the little things we often underestimate—are areas of concentration which frequently make a big difference."

The Soviet wrestler shot a desperation move and Baughman was pinned for the first time since high school. It was a lesson learned the hard way—a lesson that cost him an Olympic silver medal and one that has dogged Baughman ever since. And yet, it was the repeat of a lesson that was inflicted upon him in 1963 during his senior year in college. He was the defending NCAA champion, and was in the finals again, going for his second straight national collegiate title. He was decisioned by Jack Barden of the University of Michigan.

"It was, again, a mental breakdown that cost me," he said. "I let the anxiety build up, and I wrestled tight. A certain amount of anxiety is appropriate; but, like anything else, if you go too far with it it becomes an enemy. I was tired with anxiety exhaustion in the first fifteen seconds of the match. Then, that created more anxiety, and then that drained me even more."

Anxiety, as Baughman discovered, can work either way for an athlete. Like arousal, it can be a tremendous boost, or it can drain an athlete to a point of near total exhaustion. To be effective, it must be controlled.

"Don't be afraid of a little pregame anxiety," wrote David R. Kauss in his book *Peak Performance*. "It can really help if you don't fight it." He also noted, however, that ". . . the real task involves not avoiding or creating anxiety before competition, but using it in controlled doses. In sport, anxiety has the reputation of being both a crippler of sensitive performers and a motivator of athletes."

For Baughman, it was both. In most instances, he controlled it and employed it. In the rare cases when he lost, it controlled him.

**Wrestler Wayne Baughman, representing the United States, blocks an attempted throw by a Czechoslovakian foe by pushing on his face. The match was held in Czechoslovakia in 1963.**

"Mental preparation contributed to most of my success," he said, "and the lack of mental concentration contributed, or led directly to, those instances when I did not find success."

If mental preparation was the key to Baughman's success, what was the key to his mental preparation? Mental preparation, he insisted, can come from only one source: physical preparation. The athlete who aspires to greatness, who really demands to be the very best, must have a lock on both the mental and physical game. And the former comes only through the latter.

Vince Lombardi, the man many consider to be the finest coach in the history of professional football, provided a rare insight into the athletic mind when he uttered the statement, "Fatigue makes cowards of us all." What Lombardi meant was that any athlete, when he or she tires physically, will surrender the will to compete. The athlete does not become a coward in the true sense of the word, but a coward in the sense that he or she will begin to look for a way out, even if that way out means defeat. There comes a point when an athlete will capitulate not to the opponent but to the battle itself. The price of victory becomes too costly for the mind to support the cause. The athlete who aspires to the very top must therefore train his body, and mind, to the point that they will not, in the time limits of the sport, even approach the moment that Lombardi so eloquently addressed.

That is the true secret of unqualified athletic success.

"I don't think you can ever be mentally prepared unless you have prepared physically," said Baughman. "Gable is certainly one of the best examples of preparation. His physical and his mental preparation were equal. They went hand in hand. I have known lots of good, or great, physical specimens, but very seldom have I seen anyone who could push themselves to the upper limits, and beyond. The pain factor is there, all the time, reminding you. Blubaugh (Doug, 1960 Olympic champion) or Evans (1952 silver medalist) would be the closest in the ability to push oneself as hard as Gable."

What is the key, then, to acquiring the ability to push oneself to the uppermost limits, to face the pain barrier head on, and go through it? To what distant drummer do men like Gable, Blubaugh, Evans and Baughman march?

"The one common characteristic is the mental discipline to overcome the boredom," said Baughman. "The one item dominant in all of our Olympic champions is the fantastic, fanatical hours they put in in training."

Gable established an American precedent in wrestling with his Herculean, ongoing workouts. *Sports Illustrated* dubbed him "Superwrestler," and added that his workout program was without parallel. Chris Schenkel, commentating at the 1972 Olympics, said that Gable may have been the best conditioned athlete in the world.

Conditioning was an area of preparation that Baughman excelled in too, and he is still superbly fit, both physically and mentally. And though he no longer competes in the true sense of the word, he still relies on his confidence in his physical stamina to boost his mental toughness, just as he always has.

Consider, if you will, his training program for the Ironman Triathlon, that most gruelling of all sporting events, consisting of a two and four-tenths mile swim, a one hundred and twelve mile bike ride, and a marathon run. He doesn't have one. He simply does not go into a severe training program at all, yet he has finished three triathlons, including the world-famous event in Hawaii. He has also completed the incredibly demanding Pike's Peak Marathon, where athletes run fourteen miles up the famous mountain outside Colorado Springs, and then run fourteen miles back down, all in the thin atmosphere of the Colorado Rockies.

For such events, Baughman relies upon his "natural" shape to carry him through. It is a shape that has been carved out of nearly three decades of hard, bone-jarring workouts and an iron discipline. It is a shape that has become the essence of the man.

"I'm strictly a participant, not a competitor," he said, reflecting on his endurance performances. "I don't actually train for these things. I just try to do them in pretty much my natural condition. People ask me, 'What makes you think you can do these things?' But I was confident I was going

**Wayne Baughman sends a foe flying through the air during the 1966 Interservice Wrestling Championships. Baughman has won more national wrestling titles (sixteen) than any other matman in American history.**

to do it, although never sure how long it might take. I had no doubts that I would finish. That's the type of confidence that wrestling has given me. I know I can do anything I want to, within reason, of course."

Actually, Baughman has been wrestling and running most of his life. He has grappled with insecurity that was born in his youth and struggled with others to prove his position in a competitive world. Facing the negative reinforcement that blossomed in youth, he has reduced it to a size he can control. He has learned that the only person he must face up to, the only person that he must truly please and answer to, is the one he faces each and every morning when he gazes into the mirror. That is the fellow that Baughman, and all truly great champions, are striving to satisfy.

In his mental preparations, Baughman utilized his ability to analyze his strengths and weaknesses, and worked particularly hard and long to reduce the former and improve the latter. He also became a man of detail.

"In my situation, the ability to concentrate on the little things—the basic, fundamental things—enabled me to beat people I felt were ahead of me physically or talent-wise," he explained. "The ability to concentrate, and not to lose your composure, is often the key to winning. Those who ever watched me or Wayne Wells wrestle will see that we did not often make those little, tiny mistakes that throw a match away.

"Even when I got tired, I made sure my stance didn't get sloppy."

Mental toughness does not come quickly or easily, or arrive overnight. It's a characteristic that is developed through a long, arduous process, fashioned with demanding workouts and an even longer period of competitions and successes. But its rewards can be many.

"You learn to key in on when the other person is ready to give up," said Baughman, a man who may have lost from time to time but who has never given up. "It becomes a mind game. I can always feel the breaking point. Mental toughness is knowing you won't break before the other person does."

Lombardi would have loved Baughman, for fatigue never once made a coward of him. He trained so that fatigue became a total stranger; and, had it appeared, it is doubtful Baughman would have allowed it to enter his domain.

The story of Wayne Baughman is hardly confined to a wrestling mat. In addition to the Pike's Peak Marathon and the Ironman Triathlon, he has ridden the Hardscrabble Pass 100-mile bike race, competed in a toughman boxing competition, and climbed 28 of the 54 mountains in Colorado over 14,000 feet—with the goal of finishing the other 26 in the near future. He is proof that a man can take negative reinforcement and fashion it into a positive force—proof that a man can rise above his innermost feelings, take those hostilities and insecurities that visit us all, and channel them into a positive, constructive tool. Baughman's real success exists in his ability to conquer his sensitivities and redirect them in a manner that has earned him respect and recognition—and sixteen national wrestling titles.

**Bill Wallace displays a sword during his student days at Ball State University in Muncie, Indiana, in 1969. Wallace opened a karate club at Ball State, and earned his bachelor's degree in physical education in 1972. He also earned a master's degree from Memphis State University before becoming one of the most famed karate stars of all time.**

# BILL WALLACE

# Nice Guys Can Finish First

His fans love to call him by his nickname. And why not? This is a nation of nicknames and epithets. Americans identify and categorize most of their great sports heroes by words that represent their special skills, or that endear them to the public. John L. Sullivan was The Boston Strongboy, and George Herman Ruth was Babe. Orenthal James Simpson became O.J., or The Juice, and Julius Erving is known as Dr. J for his surgeon-like precision on a basketball court. Those two guys called Sugar Ray— Robinson and Leonard—were affectionately labelled for their sweet skills inside the boxing ring.

Bill Wallace has a nickname, too. It was applied in the martial arts arenas of the nation, and earned through an uncanny ability to lash out with his left foot in a manner that was, at the least, stunning, and, at best, unbelievable. They call him Superfoot, and with good reason. He is a phenomenon; and the foot and what he is able to do with it are a large part of that phenomenon.

When Wallace won the world professional karate championships in Los Angeles in September of 1974, *Black Belt* magazine labelled the victory "the high point of a career that is perhaps unique in the epoch of American karate." They continued, "Wallace is widely considered the number one karate fighter in the country. He is almost universally recognized as the best kicker."

But he has far more to test an opponent's defense than just his considerable kicking skills. Wallace has all the attributes to be considered one of the finest athletes ever produced in America. Consider that he has been successful in wrestling and judo, has a fine physique, and possesses lightning reflexes. Then throw in the fact that his flexibility borders on the fantastic.

Wallace is also an enigma of sorts. He is a personification of the qualities a champion must possess in order to be the very best in his field. He is tough physically and mentally, he has been blessed with a superb genetic background, and he is hungry for success. Yet, he represents a contradiction to the oft-held theory that a champion must be a vicious competitor at all times, particularly in the heat of combat.

Leo Durocher, the well-known baseball manager of several decades past, once proclaimed that "nice guys finish last." It is obvious Durocher knew nothing of Wallace (nor could he have from a chronological standpoint), for Wallace is "a nice guy" who reigned supreme as world champion for nearly six years in the rugged, often violent, always demanding world of professional karate.

Wallace's list of accomplishments in the martial arts would fill an entire page of a publicist's handout. He entered his first karate tournament at the age of nineteen, and subsequently scored six straight victories. Though he took a few lumps in the early going of his career, he quickly established himself as one of the greatest stars in the history of tournament karate.

He estimates that he has entered close to one hundred tournaments in his career, and won ninety-five percent of them. Indeed, he has captured a championship trophy from virtually every major karate tournament in America. Three times he won the United States championships, and he claimed the Top Ten national title twice. On three separate occasions, *Black Belt* magazine ranked him the number one fighter in the country, and in 1973 it added him to its Hall of Fame, where he joined such illustrious stars as Chuck Norris and Bruce Lee.

But the zenith of Wallace's karate career came in 1974 when he won the world middleweight pro karate championships. He successfully defended the title twenty-one times, scoring eleven knockouts. He retired undefeated in June of 1980 to pursue a career in the entertainment field.

Wallace can also point with pride to having competed twice, and won twice, against another legendary karate star, former world heavyweight champion Joe Lewis.

Wallace is, in the opinion of most karate practitioners and fans, one of the two or three brightest martial arts stars of all time.

"I would rank him right up there with anyone," said Terry Merriman, a Colorado Tae Kwon Do instructor who has sparred with Wallace in exhibitions. "And I think it's only a matter of time until he moves into the same class with Chuck Norris, in terms of movie successes. He's got everything it takes."

But in spite of his nearly unlimited successes, Wallace has remained a sincere and friendly man—a nice guy who never finishes last.

During a karate clinic in Fort Collins, Colorado, in the summer of 1982, Wallace showcased both his remarkable skills and his easy-going personality. While many students hung back in awe, he began his limbering

**"Superfoot" is what they call Bill Wallace, and with good cause. His kicking skills are considered by most fans the best in the history of tournament karate. Wallace taught his skills to many Hollywood stars, and once played the villain in a movie starring Chuck Norris, another of tournament karate's brightest stars.**

up procedures by asking a student to grasp one of his legs and raise it high, so that the toes actually touched the wall directly above Wallace's head while he stood with his back to that same wall. The student then brought Wallace's leg down so that it was level with his waist, and then walked the leg to the left and to the right, so that it nearly touched the wall in each direction. Moments later, Wallace dropped to the floor in a full split, and then rotated his hips, with legs stretched fully to each side, so that he could touch—easily touch, as a matter of fact—his forehead to the floor. It was a stunning display of flexibility and muscle control.

At the beginning of the seminar, Wallace led the students through a wide range of movements and techniques. He demonstrated his famous roundhouse kick, shooting his left foot to the side of a volunteer's head in lightning fashion, then holding it there for nearly two minutes as he explained the move in detail. All the time he held the foot at the ear of the student, Wallace was able to remain perfectly steady on his right foot, talking easily, not once pausing to catch his breath.

"His flexibility is almost beyond belief," said Ken Taylor, a successful high school wrestling coach and a former national placewinner. It was Taylor's first exposure to karate in general, and Wallace in particular. He was impressed.

Taylor was also stunned by two other qualities he detected in Wallace. The first was his friendly, easy-going nature; the second was his apparent inner demeanor, evidenced in a "look" in his eyes that appeared from time to time during the hour-long clinic.

As he walked around the dojo, Wallace exchanged pleasantries with the students, young and old, male and female. He sported a twinkle in his eye, and a quick smile or short, personal remark for every athlete. A man aware of his own stature, he enjoyed sharing his fame with his admirers. He was unreserved; yet, that certain look would suddenly come over him, his eyes narrowing as though he were appraising, quickly and in depth. It would linger only for a second or two, and then disappear just as quickly as it had appeared.

"He is seemingly a friendly sort of guy, a really nice guy," said an interested bystander, who had dropped in off the street in order to observe Superfoot firsthand. "But he also has that look . . . that certain something that tells you he is special, a champion, a man who knows what he is doing at all times. I guess what you'd say is he looks ready."

"Ready for what?" another asked.

"For anything," came the response.

Anything. A quick, deadly response to a threatening situation. A flurry of kicks and punches for a pressing enemy. Or, a disarming smile to a stranger who offers only friendship. Wallace is not a Sonny Liston type, you quickly sense, but a Muhammad Ali type. Like Ali, his objective is victory, not destruction. Unlike Liston, mayhem is not his priority.

"I would never go out there in a karate tournament and try to hurt someone," said Wallace after the seminar had expired and he had satisfied all the requests for autographs and small talk. "I don't want to maliciously hurt someone. I just want to give it my best shot.

"I'm friends with the guy I'm competing with. I joke with him even when I'm fighting him. There is no malice. It's just a job that I have to do. I don't get mad if I get hit a real good shot, either . . . I just want to get even. If you get something on me, then I want to get something on you."

In 1978, Wallace was called one of the "real gentlemen" in the karate world by a national magazine. "Wallace has been the outstanding star of the professional full-contact sport," it continued. "He is a combination of a joking, clowning young boy and a serious, dedicated gonna-be-somebody fighter. Since he has gone into full-contact fighting, we've never seen him out of shape or unprepared for a fight."

Those are certainly the two sides of Wallace: fun loving and friendly, and deadly serious and extremely competitive when the situation demands. Like the fabled Jack Dempsey, he has the ability to switch from personality to personality at the drop of a hat, or the raising of a fist. It is one of the keys to his popularity.

"He has that great public appeal," said promoter Mike Anderson in 1975. "In fact, he's the greatest champion I've ever seen in my life. Audiences respond to him perhaps more than to anyone else in karate."

Wallace's athletic career has included championships in wrestling and judo as well as karate. He wrestled in high school and then tried judo, winning several minor titles, before switching to karate.

"I never missed judo when I left it because I never really liked it that much," said Wallace. "I took it up after high school when I entered the service. I was pretty good at it right away, partly because of my wrestling background. But I also learned karate in the service. I realized that I could be either a good karateman, or a mediocre wrestler. Plus, my right knee was kind of mangled from wrestling."

Wallace began his karate training while serving in the Air Force in 1966 in San Bernardino, California. He didn't just ease into the sport, he attacked it with a determination that was remarkable. He would often spend several days a week, eight hours a day, in the dojo, often working until midnight. Within a year's time, he had earned his black belt.

After discharge from the Air Force, Wallace returned to his native Indiana and began working out with Glenn Kenney, to whom he credits a great deal of his sparring savvy. He also enrolled at Ball State University in Muncie, where he started a karate club and earned a bachelor of arts degree.

He then plunged headlong onto the tournament karate trail, beginning a career that would span a decade and earn him worldwide renown. The title of Superfoot would become as well known in karate circles as "the Ali Shuffle" was to boxing fans.

"The champion's real stock in trade is his incomparable legwork," said *Black Belt* magazine, "and he knows it. A typical Wallace workout starts with thirty to forty-five minutes of flexibility exercises. Then he spends a while kicking in slow motion to get his form razor sharp. The speed of his kicks generally accelerates, until the regimen is completed with 'a lot of snap kicks, concentrating on speed, movement and combinations.' "

There was a time, even at his best, when Wallace was considered primarily a kicker, a man who could come at an opponent with only one offense in mind. But despite his somewhat programmed style, the kicks were so effective that Wallace was virtually unstoppable for years. A part of his success came from the uniqueness of his style.

"My kicking techniques are basically Wallace," he told *Black Belt* magazine. "I didn't learn them from anybody. I just worked with different people on my particular abilities. I guess my hook kick is pretty much unique to me. I can use it from any position. A lot of people try to sweep me, and I can usually counter effectively with a hook kick. I use that technique both defensively and offensively, and to set up other techniques. I use a lot of double kicks, like two or three fast kicks to the face."

The Wallace offense is decidedly left-handed, as well. He is a southpaw and readily admits that nearly ninety-five percent of his offense comes from the left side, whether it be kicks, or punches.

But an opponent could not overlook the right foot, thinking it incapable of scoring. Gilbert Hansen, a nationally-known competitor in karate and bodybuilding, is just one of many who experienced the Wallace expertise from the right side.

"Bill and I fought for the overall title at a national tournament in Cincinnati in the late 1960s," said Hansen, a 230-pound bundle of pure muscle who has won dozens of bodybuilding titles and can bench press over 500 pounds. "I had won the heavyweight title and he won the middleweight title. We met for the overall, and he won.

"But three things stick out in my mind. One was that he smiles when he fights. The other is that he brought his young boy to the side of the 19 by 19 square, and sat him down. He talked real nice to him, and then turned around and fought like a tiger. He could change his mental attitude that fast."

The third thing Hansen remembers is the right foot.

"He scored with his wheel kick, and the crowd roared," said Hansen. "I disclaimed it because I didn't see it. I told the judges that they shouldn't have scored it. But everyone told me later that he did score with it . . . it was his right foot to my right ear. I just didn't see it, it was so fast. It's the only time something like that ever happened to me in all my competing. That was over fifteen years ago, and I'm impressed to this day by it."

Hansen recalled another incident when both were at a tournament. Fans and officials asked the Iowa powerhouse to flex his muscles once, like in a bodybuilding contest, and he obliged.

"Bill came up alongside me and threw a few poses, too," said Hansen, chuckling at the recollection. "You know, Bill is sinewy and well built, but he's not a musclebuilder. It was really funny and we all got a big kick out of it.

"One thing I can say is that no one likes to lose, but it's not a disgrace to lose to a man like Bill Wallace. He's really a nice guy. It's sort of like losing to Rocky Marciano, losing to someone you can really respect and like."

Wallace fully understands the necessity of drilling, technique and conditioning, and has always paid them utmost attention. But he also knows the importance of mental conditioning once an athlete has reached the uppermost levels of a sport.

"I never went into a match thinking that I might lose," he said with a smile. "People might say, 'Aren't you scared fighting in front of 10,000 people?' Sure, I'd day to myself, 'What the hell are you doing here? I could be out chasing girls.'

"But the minute that bell says 'Ding,' I'm ready. It has to be that way. It's like Rocky III—you've got to have that 'eye of the tiger,' that mental edge.

"If you've already got the expertise, the endurance, all the tools you need, you still need that mental edge to stay there. You've already trained hard, so then it's about eighty percent mental, twenty percent physical. I don't even think about it, though. Once I train myself, I know I'm ready. The number one thing that I think to myself is that there's no way this guy can beat me. I'm too fast, too strong, too smart. I may not be," he said with a quick grin, "but I tell myself that. I train hard, then I go out there for the enjoyment."

One sport that Wallace did not derive much enjoyment from, however, was professional boxing. After his appearance on ABC's "Wide World of Sports" in karate tournaments had gained him a certain degree of recognition, he decided to try his hand at boxing. He had several professional bouts, and won them all, but one negative experience drove him from the sport.

"I fought this one guy and knocked him out with a double left hook," he said, wincing at the memory. "He stayed out a long time and they took him to the hospital, and I said 'That's enough of this.' I mean, it could have been me the next time."

"That's something that people underestimate, but I can vouch for that left hook of his," said Merriman, rubbing his chin. "People think he is all foot technique, but he can really use his hands when he wants to. He stunned me pretty good with left hooks several times when we were sparring in an exhibition."

Wallace has had other career opportunities cross his path. After earning a master's degree (in kinesiology from Memphis State University) he began teaching at Memphis State in 1976, offering students instruction in judo, wrestling and karate. He also opened his own karate studio, then became a top instructor at a Memphis school co-owned by Red West, a bodyguard for and close friend of Elvis Presley.

Presley, incidentally, played a factor in Wallace's rise to super stardom in pro karate. In 1973, Wallace injured his left leg in a tournament and it failed to respond to several months of prescribed treatment. Presley heard about the injury and invited Wallace to his Graceland mansion in Memphis.

When Wallace arrived at Graceland, Presley introduced him to a Los Angeles acupuncturist Elvis had flown in.

"The guy stuck eighteen needles in my left leg, from my ankle all the way up to my hip," said Wallace. "I'll swear on a stack of Bibles, fifteen minutes after he stuck those needles in there you could kick me in that same leg and it wouldn't hurt."

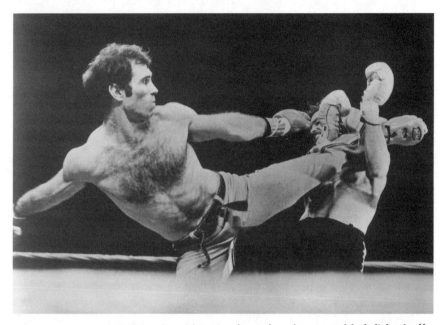

**Bill Wallace, world professional karate champion, bounces his left foot off the head of a challenger for his crown. Wallace, known as Superfoot, was 22-0 during his professional career.**

Wallace also wrote an instruction book and began offering seminars. Then he moved into the world of Hollywood.

"I found out I could make more money in one weekend doing seminars than I could in two months of teaching," said Wallace. "No wonder colleges are losing all of their people. And then I did a movie with John Belushi, and in two months made over $39,000."

The Belushi movie was "Neighbors," and it led to a longstanding friendship between Wallace and Belushi, the multitalented actor-comedian who died tragically of a drug overdose in March of 1982. Wallace gave karate instructions to Belushi, a former high school wrestler, and also served as his physical fitness consultant. He also instructed Dan Aykroyd, Belushi's close friend and co-star on the Saturday Night Live hit television show.

Wallace's movie career also included a sizeable role as a villain in the Chuck Norris vehicle, "A Force of One," and a guest star appearance in "The Manchurian."

Wallace's success in the world of karate proves that a world class athlete in the rugged world of one-on-one competition can also be a jovial, good hearted fellow—a nice guy, as it were—and still achieve the very highest levels of success.

"A person's long standing personality traits are less relevant to producing good athletic performance than are the individual states of mind, like anxiety or excitement, that the athlete can bring about at particular times for the purpose of readying," wrote David R. Kauss in *Peak Performance*.

Wallace, like Dempsey and Ali before him, has proven Durocher's theory wrong. There is room in sports for the athlete who perceives his mission as something other than a demonic pursuit of pain and destruction.

**Bruce Lee, one of the most charismatic movie stars of all time, strikes a pose in the movie "Game of Death." The martial arts superstar died in 1973 under circumstances that have yet to be explained to the satisfaction of many of his millions of fans. (Wide World Photos)**

124

# BRUCE LEE

# The Ultimate Warrior

Who is the toughest man who ever lived? If you asked that question of one hundred different people, you would probably receive one hundred different answers. Each of us has our own opinion. It may be someone we know personally—a fellow who trains at a local gym or hangs out at a local bar—or it may be someone we have seen on television. The question is, of course, academic. It can never be answered with authority or certainty, because there is no one universal and supreme measuring stick. It is not just a matter of styles (karate, judo, wrestling, boxing, etc.); it is also a question of size, dedication, desire, fortitude, and skill.

Yet, if you could somehow quiz every single person in the world, you would undoubtedly hear several names over and over. Two of these would certainly be Muhammad Ali and Bruce Lee. Ali would receive his due because he ruled the heavyweight boxing scene for much of the past twenty years, and because his name is considered to be the most recognizable in the world. His fame literally spans the entire globe, from the boroughs of New York City to the scattered huts of the most remote African villages.

Bruce Lee, on the other hand, gained his great fame in the movie houses of the world. First a product of the Orient, he later swept into the consciousness of the Western world, primarily through his fantastic performance in the movie, *Enter the Dragon*. His martial arts skills helped to ignite a karate-kung fu craze in America that still burns, though perhaps not as brightly as it did at its zenith a decade or so ago.

But Lee is as much, if not more, a mythical figure today as he was in 1973, the year he died at the age of thirty-two.

"It was Bruce Lee's function to reaffirm and exalt the masculine essence by performing over and over, with increasing charisma, the primitive ritual of mortal combat," wrote renowned biographer Albert Goldman in *Penthouse* magazine.

"No wonder, therefore, that Bruce Lee exists for millions of people as a cult figure, who is worshiped—precisely as the ancients worshiped Hercules and Achilles—as a demigod."

Goldman makes reference on several occasions to the fact that Lee was considered, in some circles, to be the deadliest man on the planet. While Goldman finally refutes that claim, the suggestion is a valid one for those caught up in the mystique of Lee. And the question—Was he the deadliest man on this planet?—remains, still unanswered ten years after his untimely and intriguing death.

Like Hercules and Achilles, Lee's life is surrounded by myth, secrecy, innuendo and rumor. Like Achilles, he is considered by many to be the ultimate warrior; the question is, does he deserve that position in the ranks of the fighting world?

Viewed as the ultimate warrior, Lee has two immediate drawbacks. The first is his size. Though he weighed in the vicinity of one hundred and fifty pounds during the beginning of his movie career, it is reported that he was closer to one hundred and thirty pounds the last several years of his life. No matter how talented and skilled Lee was, his size brings to mind the age old contention that a good big man can always defeat a good little man. Goldman stated that several of the world's top karateka scoffed at the idea that Lee could emerge victorious in combat with Ali, due largely to the great difference in their sizes (Ali fought at around 220 pounds in his prime). Joe Lewis, one of the greatest full-contact karate stars ever, made reference to Lee's size in the June, 1975 edition of *The Fighters*.

"I personally think that he would have made a relatively good fighter because of his speed," said Lewis, "but he would have never rated among top contenders because of his size. He could have been a good featherweight or lightweight (professional boxer, presumably), rated one or two in the ranks. But then he would have been obscure because most of the public's interest is focused on the heavier weights."

Lewis's evaluation of Lee's prowess as a warrior also addressed Lee's other drawback: the fact that he never competed in any official competition after his high school days when he did some boxing.

"As far as Lee goes, all anyone can say about him is that he was a great theorist and his theories—to a certain degree—work very well," said Lewis. "But then of course (there) is the fact that Bruce never fought in competition, so you can't really tell how he would have done."

Competition is the essence of the warriors' nature. Without a Hector, an Achilles is untested, and therefore unproven. Without a Joe Frazier, we would not know near as much about Ali. Without a Tunney, we could never know of Dempsey's weaknesses.

Competition taught us about Ali, Liston, Dempsey, Gable, Gotch, Hodge, Marciano, Baughman, Wallace and all the great champions of sport. It showed us—often dramatically and decisively—how they performed under the truest tests possible, and allowed us to dissect their skills, desires and strengths. Competition tells us nothing about Bruce Lee. We have only the magical and fanciful world of film to tell us of Lee's skills and ability.

Unless, of course, you accept the opinions of men who knew him, worked with him and fought with him in sparring sessions. And there are also his writings, which tell us a great deal about the man and his philosophy.

It appears that the best that can be positively said—and this is the key element of Bruce Lee's evaluation—is what Lewis told *The Fighters* in 1975: "As far as Lee goes, all anyone can say about him is that he was a great theorist and his theories—to a certain degree—work very well."

Ironically, his widow, Linda Lee, wrote that one of Bruce's favorite sayings contradicted his unwillingness to compete in karate tournaments: "Knowing is not enough, we must do," she quotes him. "Willing is not enough, we must apply."

One expert who believed in Lee's fighting abilities was Mike Stone, the karateka who gained considerable notoriety when Priscilla Presley deserted Elvis to live with him.

"For his weight, Bruce was one of the strongest people—pound for pound—I have ever met," said Stone, who used to visit Lee in Lee's home for regular workouts. "I think he could have beaten a lot of people much heavier and stronger than he was. He would have done extremely well in competition; if anything, he would have been much too fast for a lot of officials. He was that skillful."

Stone was not only impressed with Lee's skill and speed, but was also well aware of the other championship element that Lee had.

"I think Bruce would have done extremely well in a streetfighting situation because of one quality that he had: the desire to succeed and win," said Stone.

There are numerous stories of forms of competition that Lee did involve himself in. They were not the types with officials, whistles and rule books, but were street encounters with real thugs and toughs. Lee mixed it up plenty in his youth, and reportedly almost always won. Several times after he became a kung fu teacher in America, he was challenged to grudge fights—all-or-nothing affairs—by other exponents of the various arts. Again, the report suggest that he always emerged victorious. And he did not play games when he fought.

"Faced with the choice of socking your opponent in the head or poking him in the eyes, you go for the eyes every time," he once said. That should convince even the most skeptical that Bruce Lee was a fighter who played rough. He learned to play rough while growing up in the streets of Hong Kong.

". . . left idle by society, thousands of bored youth would band together into gangs and scour local neighborhoods, looking for excitement," wrote the author of an article in *Black Belt* magazine that dealt with William Cheung, a man who was notorious as a streetfighter. "Clash was inevitable. Fighting, therefore, became as much of a national pastime for a boy growing up in Hong Kong as soccer. To many, a streetwise sense of honor and pugilistic skills were the only available measures of selfworth."

The street skills of Cheung, who was a friend of Lee's and who became his sparring partner and instructor, left a large impression on Lee. The man who was to become a legendary movie star was reportedly "awed by Cheung's ability to escape unscathed from desperate circumstances. Many of Lee's students report, in fact, that throughout his life, Cheung served as Lee's mental image of the deadliest streetfighter alive. . ."

Cheung and Lee studied the kung fu style known as wing chun, instructed by the esteemed Yip Man. Short and weighing around one hundred and twenty pounds, Yip Man appeared to be anything but what he actually was—a tremendously skilled martial artist who could humble a two-hundred pounder with ease. His style was developed for women—or a man built like a woman—and was very effective, stressing mobility and evasion rather than brute force. Many of his students engaged in challenge matches on the streets, testing their skills against those of other artists. Cheung, in particular, excelled in these encounters and became something of a legend himself.

Cheung was also a master of intriguing stunts, such as standing on raw eggs without breaking them and placing a lighted cigarette on his tongue and showing no sign of pain. Years later, Lee would wow crowds with similar performances, including his famous one-inch punch. Lee would get a volunteer to hold a thick pad in front of his chest, and then place his closed fist one inch from the man's chest. After a moment's hesitation, Lee would send a hardly noticeable punch into the chest of his volunteer—from the distance of just one inch—and send the volunteer sprawling to the ground.

Writing about his childhood in Hong Kong and his involvement with various street gangs, Linda described her husband as "a fighter first and foremost and everything else afterwards." She wrote, "He was a born competitor."

He was also a born student—at least in one area. In fact, it is doubtful that any other man has made a more complete study of the fighting arts. He was insatiable when it came to analyzing the elements of a warrior's various methods and techniques. He may have been the greatest student of one-on-one competition ever to live.

Danny Inosanto, one of Lee's closest confidants, claimed that Lee had one of the largest collections of fight films every assembled, and would study them for up to nine hours at a crack.

"Muhammad Ali was probably his favorite fighter, but Bruce took something from everybody," said Inosanto. "He liked Ali's footwork and admired his outside fighting. He liked Marciano's short punches. He used to study all the knockout punches of Joe Louis. Ray Robinson—his moves, his bobs and weaves. He liked them all, and they all had fine points that he borrowed and perfected."

Richard Bustillo, another of Lee's disciples, explained that Lee was after knowledge of all the fighting arts.

"Boxing, western fencing, wrestling—Bruce Lee studied them all. In each was a kernel of the truth he was trying to demonstrate. The totality is Bruce's art."

In his eagerness to learn, Lee would try any fighting form, any art. He was a man in search of the ultimate truth, and he recognized that no particular form, whether it be karate, kung fu, boxing or wrestling, in and of itself was all encompassing. He borrowed the properties from each discipline that would make for the total warrior. He combined them all, taking from each what was good, and discarding from each what was, in his opinion, ineffective. He was interested in karate for striking from a distance, boxing for the hand technqiues that in-close fighting required, and wrestling or judo for the combat that would ensue if the two combatants were to lock horns.

"His theory of training was through self-discovery," said Inosanto. "He'd spar with anybody he could. All his technique was derived through self discovery. He used to call it 'discovering the source of your ignorance.' Anybody who would visit him—and he had a lot of visitors from the karate world—he'd spar with them, with or without gloves, either way."

Perhaps Lee's greatest attribute was his willingness to search for the truth, and then incorporate the truth when he discovered it. In his absorbing and comprehensive book, *Tao of Jeet Kune Do*, he opens with a statement that best defines his philosophy.

"This book is dedicated to the free, creative martial artist," he wrote. "Take what is useful and develop from there." At that, Lee was the master.

"In his lifelong quest for self-knowledge and personal expression, Bruce was constantly studying, analyzing and modifying all available relative information," wrote Linda Lee. "His principle source was his personal library which consisted of over two thousand books dealing with all forms of physical conditioning, martial arts, fighting techniques and related subjects."

Lee studied practically every form of fighting and then developed his own style, calling it Jeet Kune Do. It departed from the traditional martial arts in that it was devoid of most of the forms and katas, and dealt almost exclusively with practicality and application. Lee was far more concerned with the functional than the traditional aspect of the arts.

**The legendary Bruce Lee (left) fends off a kick by Kareem Abdul-Jabbar in the movie "Game of Death." Lee, considered by many the greatest martial artist of all time, once had Jabbar, one of the greatest basketball players ever, as a student in his martial arts class, and invited him to play a villain in the movie. (Wide World Photos)**

Lee moved from Hong Kong to San Francisco late in his teens, and eventually wound up at the University of Washington in Seattle, where he studied philosophy. He then moved back down the coast, and began teaching Jeet Kune Do. Among his students were such personalities as Kareem Abdul-Jabbar, James Coburn and Steve McQueen. He left an impression on all of them.

"Bruce was the Nuygen, the Nijinsky, of martial arts," Coburn said shortly after Lee's death. "He could do it. He could do all that stuff that was on film, whereas with the other guys, everything is done in quick cuts and a lot of movie tricks. Bruce really did them. To watch his work was amazing."

John Saxon, who starred with Lee in *Enter the Dragon*, was most impressed with Lee's ability to absorb knowledge and implement it quickly.

"As a martial artist—which is what Bruce considered himself first and foremost—he was very innovative," said Saxon. "He was able to see the potential weaknesses and defects of any particular system. Therefore, he joined many things together . . ."

Another of the stars of *Enter the Dragon* was Jim Kelly, who earned a strong reputation in tournament karate before turning to the celluloid kind. He was a maverick, so to speak, in that he studied not only karate, but boxing, wrestling and judo, incorporating all the best of each. And, he said, ". . . I found that Bruce did the same thing."

Lee's passion for the fighting arts was matched by his zeal for conditioning. He considered running extremely important, and also trained with weights. His earliest martial arts movies, *Fists of Fury* and *The Chinese Connection*, show a Bruce Lee that weighed around one-hundred and fifty pounds, with exceptional muscular development. His lat spread was tremendous for a man of his size, and the muscles on his body rippled with each movement. He was also adept at muscular control—as evidenced in the movie *Return of the Dragon*, in which he rotates his shoulder blades in a most bizarre fashion.

When he became financially comfortable, Lee outfitted his home with a huge gymnasium, one that was nearly as large as one you would find in a good-sized college. In addition, his home was peppered with various apparatus for sparring and testing reflexes and techniques. Linda reported that he became nearly obsessed with fitness and techniques, and was constantly working out in some fashion.

He was well known for his variations of pushups, and was able to do not only one-handed pushups, but one-fingered pushups. He would also do pushups while using only his thumbs for support.

In addition to being incredibly strong for his size, Lee had amazing flexibility. He could leap high off the ground, completely spread-eagle his legs,and touch his feet with his hands while in mid-air. He was also a skilled gymnast, capable of acrobatic feats that would have impressed any top college gymnast.

He developed his forearm muscles by holding a seventy-pound barbell at arms' length straight out from his chest, and he used to work out with a pair of dumbbells while watching television. He had several punching bags of various dimensions hanging from his ceilings, and was constantly kicking and punching them.

Lee also brought two other components into a fight: he was a fierce competitor, and he had an unrelenting pride. Both are essential ingredients of a champion. But his biggest advantage, as Lewis pointed out, was his blinding speed.

"His speed was literally unbelievable," said Herb Jackson, a former student. "He could hit you before you could even see him do it. He had to slow himself down for the cameras in his pictures as well as allow for reaction time from the stuntmen or actors."

Linda also offers testimony of his incredible speed: "Time and again I watched some of the greatest martial arts experts in America left flailing wildly as Bruce jabbed towards their faces and bodies; personally, I never saw anyone block him." Yet the occasions were, once again, exhibitions put on by Lee, and not actual combats.

The essence of Bruce Lee as a warrior revolved around his knowledge of all styles, his adaptability to all styles, and his dedication to training and physical conditioning. In the latter respect, he is rivaled only by Rocky Marciano and Dan Gable, two men who are recognized as the greatest trainers ever in their respective fields of boxing and wrestling. Lee fits that same mold.

"No other human being had ever trained the way Bruce trained— fanatically," said Chuck Norris shortly after Lee's death. "He lived and breathed it from the time he got up at six o'clock in the morning until he went to bed at night. He was either working out or thinking about it. His mind was always active, never resting. He was always thinking about what he could do to improve himself . . ."

Norris, one of tournament karate's brightest stars ever and now the king of the martial arts films, had nothing but praise for Lee in a memorial edition released by O'Hare Publications in 1973. He said he considered Lee to be pound-for-pound the strongest man in the world.

Today, more than ten years after his death, Lee still has a fanatical hold on his legions of devoted fans. They include movie stars, famous athletes, karate practitioners, alley fighters and just plain common folks.

He captured the imagination of such diverse athletes as Kareem Abdul-Jabbar, one of the brightest stars in the history of basketball, Randy Lewis, a four-time All-American wrestler at the University of Iowa and a member of the 1980 Olympic wrestling team, and Lou Ferrigno, the former Mr. Universe bodybuilding champion who starred on television as The Incredible Hulk.

"I have seen *Enter the Dragon* at least twenty-two times," said Ferrigno shortly after completing filming of his first Hercules movie. "I think if Bruce Lee had lived, he would have been one of the two or three biggest movie stars in the world, like Burt Reynolds. He had that certain charisma, that something special. But I did wonder if he could really do all that stuff he did on film, or if a lot of it was merely theatrics."

Jabbar studied under Lee for a brief time, and Lewis is an ardent fan who never overlooks the opportunity to see one of his movies or discuss his skills. Theirs is an admiration shared by a great many athletes, in a wide range of sports, all of whom are mesmerized by the exciting, charismatic force that leaps onto the screen with dynamic presence whenever a Bruce Lee movie is shown.

There is yet another, final link between Lee and the great heroes of antiquity. Like Achilles, Lee was considered indestructible by many of his followers. The Greeks attributed Achilles' invincibility to a precaution his mother took at his birth. Holding him by the heel, she dipped his body into the River Styx, the river that flows through Hades, and made him nearly immortal. According to legend, he could be killed only by a wound to his

**Is this the face of the ultimate warrior, the greatest fighting machine this planet has ever known? Bruce Lee's stature has been compared to that of a Hercules or Achilles, two of the mythological heroes of ancient Greece. (Wide world Photos)**

heel. It took a poisoned arrow from the bow of the Trojan warrior, Paris, to slay Achilles; it struck him in the heel, his only vulnerable spot.

The essence of the supreme heroes is that they can never be overcome by ordinary means. So it was with Lee, and rumors surrounding his death are as mystical as those surrounding the death of Achilles. The martial arts world is riddled with bizarre stories revolving around the mythical and feared "delayed death touch"—also known as "the vibrating palm" and "dim mak." The June 1975 issue of *Oriental Fighting Arts* magazine contained a story entitled "The Death Touch and Bruce Lee," suggesting that Lee may have been killed by the mysterious technique. The article even offered diagrams to show how the "touch" works. It is a theory embraced whole-heartedly by many, and scoffed at by others. It's major impact, however, is that it catapulted Lee into the same mythical world that is inhabited by Achilles. Warriors of the mold of Bruce Lee and Achilles can, afterall, only be killed in the most mysterious and unexplained fashions if they are to become objects of cults and hero worship.

To many, Lee was the ultimate warrior, the greatest fighting machine ever born. Whether or not this was true is highly debatable because he chose not to prove himself and his fighting abilities in actual competition. This much remains certain, however: Lee possessed all the necessary ingredients to be one of this planet's most proficient warriors, and one of its toughest men. There is no question as to his incredible speed, his unwavering dedication, his great physical strength, and his extraordinary pride and competitiveness. Only his skill is debatable, because it was never proven in the sports arena. But no one questions his knowledge, and the years he spent accumulating it. Bruce Lee may or may not have been the ultimate warrior, but he was, it seems safe to say, the ultimate student of the ways of the warrior.

# Biographical Sketches of The Toughest Men in Sports

MUHAMMAD ALI:

Born January 17, 1942, in Louisville, Kentucky (as Cassius Marcellus Clay, Jr.), Muhammad Ali was heavyweight boxing champion of the world three times: from February 25, 1964 until being stripped of the title in the summer of 1967 for refusing military induction; from October 30, 1974, until February 15, 1978; and from September 15, 1978, until his temporary retirement in 1979. Ring record: 61 bouts; 56 victories, including 37 knockouts. He lost four by decision, and was stopped once when he failed to answer the bell for the eleventh round against Larry Holmes. His amateur record was 98-6 and included several national titles, plus a gold medal in the 1960 Olympics in the light-heavyweight class. At his peak, Ali stood six foot three inches and weighed around 215 pounds.

WAYNE BAUGHMAN:

Born January 4, 1941, in Oklahoma City, Oklahoma, Wayne Baughman won a total of 16 national wrestling titles and was national sombo (Russian judo) champion in 1976. He was 1967 Pan-American Games champion and placed in world competition on several different occasions. His complete amateur wrestling record is unavailable, but he competed in 25 national tournaments and never placed lower than third. He competed mostly in the 190-pound class, and stood six foot, two inches tall. Baughman is a member of the Helms Foundation Wrestling Hall of Fame, and the United States Wrestling Federation Hall of Fame.

JACK DEMPSEY: Born June 24, 1895, in Manassa, Colorado, Jack Dempsey was heavyweight boxing champion of the world from July 4, 1919, until September 23, 1926. Ring record: 80 official bouts; 60 victories, including 49 knockouts. He had 7 draws, and 6 other bouts where no decision was rendered. He lost 6 times by decision, once by knockout. At his peak, Dempsey weighed 187 pounds and was six foot and three-fourths inches tall. He engaged in many boxing exhibitions and scored many more "unofficial" knockouts. Died May 31, 1983, in New York City from natural causes at age 87. Elected to Boxing Hall of Fame in 1954.

ROBERTO DURAN: Born June 16, 1951, in Guarare, Panama, Roberto Duran was lightweight boxing champion of the world from June 26, 1972, until giving up the title in 1980 to move up in weight. He was welterweight boxing champion of the world from June 20, 1980, until November 25, 1980. Won junior middleweight crown June 16, 1983, to become one of just six men in boxing history to hold 3 world titles. Ring record (through May, 1983): 80 official fights; 76 victories, including 56 knockouts. He lost three times by decision, and once when he quit in the middle of the eighth round in a 1980 fight with Ray Leonard, surrendering his title. Duran is five feet seven inches tall and fought as a professional from 135 pound to 154 pounds. His amateur record is unknown.

DAN GABLE:    Born October 25, 1948, in Waterloo, Iowa, Dan Gable was the 149.5 pound world amateur wrestling champion in 1971 and 1972 (the latter at the Munich Olympics). He won 180 straight matches in high school and college, and won five national championships and six straight titles at the Midlands, which is considered America's toughest meet. His entire amateur record was 305 wins, 7 losses. Gable is five foot nine inches tall. He is a member of the Helms Foundation Wrestling Hall of Fame, the United States Wrestling Federation Hall of Fame and the Iowa Wrestling Hall of Fame.

FRANK GOTCH:    Born April 27, 1878, on a farm near Humboldt, Iowa, Frank Gotch was the world heavyweight professional wrestling champion from April 3, 1908, until his retirement in the summer of 1915. His official record is sketchy, but the best estimate is that he was 394-6, and wrestled several hundred exhibitions without losing once. At his peak, Gotch was five feet, eleven and one half inches tall, and weighed 212 pounds. Though there is no official professional wrestling hall of fame, Gotch is considered by most experts to be the greatest professional wrestler of all time. He died December 16, 1917, at the age of 40 from uremic poisoning.

DAN HODGE:

Born May 13, 1932, on a farm near Perry, Oklahoma, Dan Hodge is one of only two men to ever win national titles in both boxing and wrestling. He was a seven-time national wrestling champion (NCAA, freestyle and Greco-Roman) between 1953 and 1957, and placed second in the 1956 Olympics. He won the national AAU heavyweight boxing championship in 1959. As an amateur, Hodge wrestled between 174 and 177 pounds and stood just under six-foot tall. He was 8-2 as a professional boxer, and wrestled professionally for many years. College wrestling record: 46 wins, no losses. He was 96-3 in high school and college, and his total amateur wrestling record is unavailable. He is a member of the Helms Wrestling Hall of Fame and the United States Wrestling Federation Hall of Fame.

BRUCE LEE:

Born November 27, 1940, in San Francisco, California, Bruce Lee participated in no official competition, other than a boxing tournament in high school in Hong Kong, which he won. He made a total of six motion pictures, including two as a child star in Hong Kong, and was involved with four more movies that were released after his death. He also played Kato on the Green Hornet television series in 1966-67. His most successful and important movie was *Enter The Dragon*, which was released in 1973 just shortly after his death. Lee was five-foot seven inches tall and his weight fluctuated between 137 and 155 pounds as an adult. He died July 20, 1973, in Hong Kong at the age of 32. The official autopsy lists the cause of death as brain swelling brought on by the use of aspirin. Lee was voted into *Black Belt* Magazine's Hall of Fame in 1974.

ROCKY MARCIANO:    Born September 1, 1923, in Brockton, Massa-chusetts, Rocky Marciano was heavyweight boxing champion of the world from September 23, 1952, until April 27, 1956. Ring record: 49 professional fights; 49 victories, including 43 knockouts. As an amateur his record was 8-4. At his peak, Marciano weighed 184 pounds and was five foot, eleven inches tall. He was killed in a plane crash near Newton, Iowa, on August 31, 1969, the day before his 46th birthday. He was elected to the Boxing Hall of Fame in 1959.

GENE TUNNEY:    Born May 25, 1897, in New York City, New York, Gene Tunney was heavyweight boxing champion of the world from September 23, 1926, until July 27, 1928. Ring record: 77 official bouts; 57 victories, including 42 knock-outs. He had one draw, and 18 other fights where no decision was rendered. Tunney lost one fight by decision and was never knocked out. He was very successful as an amateur, but the record is incomplete. At his peak, Tunney weighed 192 pounds and stood six foot and one half inches tall. He died on November 7, 1978, at Greenwich, Connecticut, from natural causes at the age of 81. He was elected to the Boxing Hall of Fame in 1955.

BILL WALLACE:

Born December 1, 1937, in Portland, Indiana, Bill Wallace was middleweight karate champion of the world from September of 1974 until June of 1980 when he retired undefeated. Though his overall record is unknown, he was 22-0, with 11 knockouts, as champion. During his career, he won virtually every major karate tournament in America and was selected by *Black Belt* magazine as the top fighter in the country three times. He entered his first tournament in 1956 and has won 95 percent of the 75 to 100 tournaments he has competed in. At his peak, Wallace weighed 165 pounds and stood five foot, ten inches tall. He was named to the *Black Belt* Magazine Hall of Fame in 1973.

# POSTSCRIPT

"I've made a lifelong study in psychology, because it's in the mind where you separate the winners from the losers," said Hayden Fry, football coach at the University of Iowa, recently.

Fry's great knowledge about athletic performance is evident from his record. He has taken football programs that were at rock-bottom at three different colleges—Southern Methodist University, North Texas State and Iowa—and turned them rapidly into winners. Iowa had not known a winning season for twenty consecutive years when Fry arrived on campus, yet in just his third season the Hawkeyes finished 8-3, won the Big Ten Conference championship and played in the Rose Bowl. The following season, in 1982, Iowa fashioned an overall record of 8-4, which included a Peach Bowl victory over the University of Tennessee.

"I have never coached anyplace where motivation wasn't extremely important," added Fry in an article written by Buck Turnbull for the *Des Moines Register*. "We spend a lot of time trying to analyze each individual personality on the team. We're searching for what you might call sensitivities—things that turn people on, and things that turn them off."

The secret to overwhelming athletic success lies in the recesses of the mind, and in mental preparation. More and more, as athletes and coaches strive for excellence, they are turning inward, trying to latch onto the secrets that will unlock the door to success. There are a number of keys that will open the door. As shown through the experiences of the great champions in the preceding chapters, there are many and varied reasons for athletic success and failure. While a lack of fear sustained Rocky Marciano, the ability to deal with deep and gnawing fears boosted Jack Dempsey and Gene Tunney to the very top. Working himself into a state of high arousal was essential for Muhammad Ali, and Roberto

Duran won with anger as an ally. Wayne Baughman grappled with negative feelings, and was able to convert them into positive reinforcement. Dan Gable's dedication and total commitment to a goal sent him to the pinnacle of his world, and Bill Wallace provided ample proof that any personality type can compete successfully in the violent world of one-on-one competition. Confidence was the major factor in the successes of Frank Gotch, and Dan Hodge demonstrated that a man can be versatile enough to excel in two demanding sports like boxing and wrestling. For Bruce Lee, success was wrapped up in his unrelenting pursuit of knowledge and perfection.

All of these men's stories possess elements of truth that an aspiring athlete can benefit from if they are applied to his or her own set of circumstances. But after all is said and done, the single most important element in the success story of an athlete is the desire to excel. It is up to each individual athlete to assess his or her own abilities and determine which qualities are present and which are lacking. A decision must then be made. Is the necessary work that lies ahead worth the price? Will the ends justify the means?

Anrold Schwarzenegger, arguably the best bodybuilder of all time, didn't mince words when he discussed what it takes to be among the best bodybuilders in the world. According to Schwarzenegger, an athlete must be able to blast through the pain barrier and accept the pain that goes with it. In the movie, *Pumping Iron*, Schwarzenegger said, ". . . repetitions, that's what makes the muscles grow, that's what divides the champions from not being champions. If one can go through this pain barrier, you may get to be a champion. If you can't go through it, forget it.

"And that's what most people lack . . . is having the guts to go in and say, 'I go through and I don't care what happens. It aches and if I fall down—I have no fear of fainting in the gym. I know it can happen . . . I threw up many times while working out, but is doesn't matter, because *it's all worth it.*' "

Each of the men in this book faced a similar decision and moved past it without pausing to look back. And they may be unique, but they are not without similarities. Their common bond is their courage, their commitment, their desire, and their ability to see that desire through to the very end. There are many other athletes who could have been in this book. Those selected are merely examples the author is most familiar with and partial to. The important element of their selection is the message they relay, individually and collectively, and it is this: If you are willing to move through the pain barriers, and if you are willing to pay the price, then you too can taste the sweet nectar that flows from athletic success.

# ABOUT THE AUTHOR

Mike Chapman has been a professional journalist for nearly fifteen years. Currently the sports editor of the *Cedar Rapids Gazette*, Iowa's second largest newspaper, he is the author of four books and has had articles appear in nine national magazines, including *Black Belt*, *Karate Illustrated*, *Strength & Health* and *The Olympian*. He was named winner of the Bob Dellinger Award as national wrestling writer of the year 1976 by *Amateur Wrestling News*, and in 1982 *Wrestling USA* selected him Sportswriter of the Year. His novel, *GOTCH*, was picked as Book of the Year in 1981 by the Broome Agency of Florida, and won a cash award of $1,250. Chapman has been involved in weight training on a regular basis for over twenty years, and is a regular jogger. He has competed in such sports as wrestling, judo and sambo. He and his wife, Bev, have three children: Jacquie, Jenny and Jason.